The Creative Curriculum® for Preschool, Fifth Edition

Volume 4: Mathematics

Juanita V. Copley, Candy Jones, Judith Dighe

Contributing Authors:
Toni S. Bickart and Cate Heroman

 **Teaching**Strategies® · Washington, D.C.

English editing: Laurie Taub, Toni S. Bickart, and Judith F. Wohlberg
Design and layout: Jeff Cross, Amy Jackson, Abner Nieves, Judy Myers, Auburn & Associates
Spanish translation: Claudia Caicedo Núñez
Spanish editing: Renée Fendrich, Judith F. Wohlberg
Illustrations: Jennifer Barrett O'Connell
Cover design: Laura Monger Design

Teaching Strategies, Inc.
P.O. Box 42243
Washington, DC 20015

www.TeachingStrategies.com

978-1-60617-372-5

Teaching Strategies and *The Creative Curriculum* names and logos are registered trademarks of Teaching Strategies, Inc., Washington, D.C. Brand-name products of other companies are given for illustrative purposes only and are not required for implementation of the curriculum.

Library of Congress Cataloging-in-Publication Data

The creative curriculum for preschool : volume 1 : the foundation / Diane Trister Dodge ... [et al.] ; Kai-leé Berke, contributing author. -- 5th ed.
      p. cm.
  Prev. ed. cataloged under Dodge, Diane Trister.
  Includes bibliographical references and index.
  ISBN 978-1-60617-369-5 (v. 1 : alk. paper) -- ISBN 978-1-60617-370-1 (v. 2 : alk. paper) -- ISBN 978-1-60617-371-8 (v. 3 : alk. paper) -- ISBN 978-1-60617-372-5 (v. 4 : alk. paper) -- ISBN 978-1-60617-373-2 (v. 5 : alk. paper) 1. Education, Preschool--Curricula--United States. 2. Child care--United States. 3. Early childhood education--Curricula. 4. Preschool children--Services for. 5. Curriculum planning--United States. 6. Child development--United States. I. Dodge, Diane Trister. II. Dodge, Diane Trister Creative curriculum for preschool.

  LB1140.4.D633 2010
  372.19--dc22
                                        2010021778
1 2 3 4 5 6 7 8 9 10   17 16 15 14 13 12 11 10
      Printing   Year Printed

Printed and bound in United States of America

Acknowledgments

We received much help from many talented people. We want to thank our expert panel for their work in reviewing our drafts and providing specific feedback and suggestions:

Rosalind Charlesworth, Ph.D., Professor and Chair, Department of Child and Family Studies, Weber State University, Ogden, UT

Laura Colker, Ph.D., early childhood education consultant and co-author of *The Creative Curriculum for Preschool*, Washington, DC

Nell W. McAnelly, M.Ed., Associate Director, Gordon A. Cain Center for Scientific, Technological, Engineering, and Mathematical Literacy, Louisiana State University

Roberta McHardy, Ph.D., Assistant Professor, Department of Educational Theory, Policy, and Practice, Louisiana State University, Baton Rouge, LA

Lois Rector, M.Ed., early childhood education consultant, member of the Teaching Strategies Staff Development Network, Slaughter, LA

Walter Rosenkrantz, Ph.D., Professor Emeritus, Department of Mathematics and Statistics, University of Massachusetts (Amherst), Amherst, MA

Toni S. Bickart and Cate Heroman of Teaching Strategies provided so much help that we are delighted to list them as contributing authors. We also thank Sue Mistrett, who gave us particular guidance about adaptations to the Computer area.

Thanks to Margot Ziperman, Production Manager, for her excellent handling of the design and production process and to Abner Nieves and Jeff Cross for their imaginative design, careful layout, and senses of humor. We thank Laurie Taub and Judy Wohlberg for their editing and Rachel Friedlander Tickner for her diligent copy editing.

Over the last 6 years we have introduced the concepts in this book to hundreds of teachers who have used them with many groups of children. We thank all of them for their commitment and hard work.

We thank Diane Trister Dodge, President and Founder of Teaching Strategies, for her continuing support and encouragement.

Table of Contents

How to Use This Book

The Creative Curriculum for Preschool, Volume 4: Mathematics is an important part of Teaching Strategies' mathematics program. While teachers can use the book by itself, it is a valuable part of a comprehensive curriculum and assessment system for children ages 3–5. This volume expands on the information in *Volume 1: The Foundation* to show how and why mathematics can and should be part of children's everyday experiences and activities. It explains early mathematics learning and describes when and how to teach directly the skills and concepts children need to become successful mathematical thinkers.

Chapter 21, The Components of Mathematics, describes preschool mathematics content: 1) number and operations, 2) geometry and spatial sense, 3) measurement, 4) patterns [algebra], and 5) data analysis. This chapter explains the concepts involved, summarizes related research, gives explicit guidance about ways in which teachers intentionally promote children's understanding of the concepts, and offers suggestions for assessing children's learning. It includes "Tips to Share With Families," which offers ideas for supporting children's mathematics learning at home.

Chapter 22, Mathematical Process Skills, describes the five process skills of mathematics: 1) problem solving, 2) reasoning, 3) communicating, 4) connecting, and 5) representing. The chapter shows how teachers can intentionally promote children's acquisition of each skill. A sample classroom activity illustrates ways to encourage children to use each process skill presented, to help teachers clearly understand how to teach the skill.

Chapter 23, Planning Your Mathematics Program, helps you get started. To plan, you have to know what you want children to learn. This chapter therefore begins with an at-a-glance list of *The Creative Curriculum® for Preschool* objectives for development and learning, including the four objectives that are directly related to mathematics. They guide your observation and planning, so references to these objectives are made throughout the book. The developmental progression for each of the mathematics objectives is included in the appendix of this volume.

Because the physical environment has a powerful effect on children's development and learning, we explain how to create a mathematically rich classroom that includes a wide range of materials that encourage children to explore mathematics. We show how every event in the day, from children's arrival to their departure, is an opportunity to promote mathematics learning.

The next section of this chapter describes how teachers offer learning opportunities for large and small groups during planned, teacher-guided instructional experiences. We also show how long-term studies give children meaningful opportunities to use mathematics. Because some children have special needs, this chapter offers guidance about meeting the particular strengths and needs of English-language learners, advanced mathematics learners, and children with disabilities.

Chapter 24, Mathematics Learning in Interest Areas and Outdoors, invites you to reconsider interest areas and the outdoors as the context for mathematics learning. The chapter begins with a discussion of the Toys and Games area, which is the hub of mathematics learning in *The Creative Curriculum* classroom. The discussions of the remaining ten interest areas are formatted in the same way. The first section of each discussion examines everyday experiences that typically occur in the area and shows the relationship to mathematics. As you evaluate your interest areas and outdoor area, use the suggestions in this chapter to include mathematics-related materials and books. There are suggestions about how to scaffold children's learning as they engage in everyday experiences in the area. A final section helps you observe children's progress while working in the area.

The Creative Curriculum for Preschool, Volume 4: Mathematics can be used in a variety of ways. Teachers can use it independently to broaden their understanding of mathematics for young children and to find appropriate instructional strategies. It can also serve as the content for focused professional development efforts, either in study groups or learning teams, or as part of ongoing training. Teachers could learn about a specific component and related strategies and then practice them in the classroom. These classroom experiences can be discussed with colleagues at later sessions. In addition, teacher mentors can model a particular strategy, demonstrate how the major components of mathematics are addressed, and then coach teachers in their use of the techniques explained in this book.

Components of Mathematics

Components of Mathematics

Through observation of young children, we have come to know and understand that mathematics is already a part of their world—and they love it! A 1-year-old asks for more cookies and cries when someone takes one away. Two-year-olds display two fingers to tell how old they are. Three-year-olds use geometry skills as they rotate and stack blocks to form tall towers. Four-year-olds identify patterns in the floor tile and predict what will happen when they turn the corner. Five-year-olds are fascinated with how tall they are and how their height compares to that of a *Tyrannosaurus rex*.

Research supports the notion that young children have an intuitive sense of informal mathematics. It can be seen during play when they use mathematics to make sense of their world. Numerically, young children count coins as they shop at the store, write numbers to help them remember how many orders of flowers a pretend customer wants, and use a number sequence as they exercise in a pretend aerobics class. Geometrically, children manipulate puzzle pieces, use positional words when they enact the *Three Billy Goats Gruff*, and investigate shapes as they build a city in the Block area. Algebraically, children create patterns in their art work and march in rhythm to a song. From a measurement perspective, they build tall structures and compare them to friends' structures, or they weigh fruit at the class supermarket. Indeed, the skills children learn and use during creative, imaginative play easily involve mathematical concepts.

As an early childhood teacher, you play an important role in bridging children's informal understanding of mathematics with more formal, school-based mathematics. That is, you design the learning environment by purposely placing mathematics materials in interest areas for child-initiated explorations and by intentionally introducing activities with a mathematics focus. You observe and listen as children interact with materials and their peers, and then you use mathematical vocabulary to describe their actions and thinking. You ask questions as children investigate. You play logic games, create mathematical problem-solving stories, and include numerical and algebraic activities as part of the daily routine.

The National Council of Teachers of Mathematics crafted content standards in five areas for prekindergarten children:

- number and operations

- geometry and spatial sense

- measurement

- patterns (algebra)

- data analysis

These standards are described in *Principles and Standards for School Mathematics* (NCTM, 2000) and were used to organize discussions of mathematics in *The Creative Curriculum for Preschool*. The NCTM publication *Curriculum Focal Points* (2006) confirms that number and operations, geometry, and measurement are the areas that should receive the most emphasis in preschool.

This chapter discusses each component in more detail, relating research to the teacher's role and to assessment strategies. With a clear understanding of the components of mathematics, teachers will be able to observe children, analyze and evaluate their mathematics learning and development, and plan instruction to help each child progress.

Number and Operations

Number concepts are the most easily identified mathematical content in early childhood classrooms. In fact, young children often say, when asked about math, "It's about numbers and counting." Without doubt, number is the most important and usable concept for young children and is the concept that should receive the most emphasis in the preschool classroom. At the preschool level, number and operations concepts involve nine different ideas.

Counting

To count well, children must learn three things: the number sequence, one-to-one correspondence, and that the last number named when counting a set of objects tells *how many* are in the set. The first 20 numbers in the *counting sequence* are usually learned by rote. Young preschoolers first learn to understand the words *one, two, three, four* and to identify collections of objects that represent those numbers. Older preschoolers may count to 10 and beyond, but they may not do so consistently or in the correct order. When children hear larger numbers such as the 30s, 40s, or 50s, they begin to understand the pattern of number names and counting becomes easier. Because number names like *eleven, twelve,* and *thirteen* do not follow a typical pattern like *twenty-one, twenty-two,* and *twenty-three,* they can be especially troublesome.

One-to-one correspondence means that one number name is given or matched to one and only one object in a set being counted. One-to-one correspondence is important in helping children keep track of the objects they have or have not counted in a set. Finally, children must realize that the last number named when all objects in a set have been counted is the number that tells *how many.* This is called the *cardinal number.* For example, after a child counts four pennies, he says, "I have four pennies," and does not start the counting sequence again.

Quantity (Sense of Number)

Understanding how many are in a set is one of the first number ideas a child demonstrates. When asked how old she is, a young child may incorrectly show two fingers and say, "Three," or extend three fingers and say, "Two." With experience, children easily develop a sense of number about objects in small sets, that is, sets with two, three, or four objects. Children can often look at a group of objects or fingers extended on one hand and identify the quantity without even counting. This is referred to as *subitizing.* In most instances, however, young children develop an understanding of quantity by counting the objects in a set or making a specific set of objects.

Comparisons (More–Fewer or More–Less)

When comparing two sets, children can often tell which set has more or less by simply looking. They can also match the individual items in the sets to determine which set has more or which set has fewer. At an early age, children should be able to use words like *one more* or *two more.* The words *fewer* and *less* are seldom part of children's everyday vocabulary. However, they often use words that have the same meaning, such as *littler* or *not as much* to talk about the set containing fewer items.

Order

Ordinal numbers—*first, second, third*, and so forth—indicate sequence. Common uses of these words indicate where someone is in line or the position of items in a row of objects. Most young children have no problem understanding the concept of first; the other ordinal numbers are more difficult.

Numerals

Just as young children need to learn about alphabet letters and how to write them, they also need to investigate the use of numerals. Writing numerals is not an important skill at the preschool level, but children should see numerals displayed, begin to develop an understanding of what they represent, and investigate their use.

Combining Operations (Adding)

While young children are not adding with symbols in the traditional sense, they often combine sets of objects to find out *how many in all*. Common word problems for children involve getting more of something and then finding out how many they have all together. They also combine sets of objects to make a larger set.

Separating Operations (Subtracting)

The operation of *take away* is a common separating operation and one that young children understand. A common separating problem is one that involves a child's having a set of objects and removing some objects. The child then finds out how many *are left*.

Sharing Operations (Dividing)

Young children grow up *sharing* snacks, coins, and small toys. When they begin with a set of objects and *share* them with friends, they are beginning to understand the operation of dividing, or forming groups. In working with young children, the concept of a *fair share* must to be taught and emphasized.

Set-Making Operations (Multiplying)

Children begin to develop an understanding of multiplication when they engage in activities such as distributing birthday treats or passing out materials. For example, they make equal sets when they give everyone two cookies or four crayons, or when they place three pieces of plastic eating utensils at each place setting in the Dramatic Play area.

What Does Research Say?

Children develop counting skills at very early ages. The easiest collections for a 3-year-old to count are those in a straight line. From 3 to 5 years of age, children learn to count objects in larger sets and in different arrangements (Baroody, 2004).

Many 3-year-old children believe that two sets of objects have the same number if the objects are close to each other. By age 4, many children can develop a matching process so that they can compare the sets (Piaget & Szeminska, 1952).

Three- and 4-year-old children can often solve subtraction problems before they can solve addition problems (Copley & Hawkins, 2005).

Three-year-olds can divide small collections into equal subsets. Many 4- and 5-year-olds can divide larger collections by using specific sharing strategies (Clements, 2004).

To solve combining or separating problems, young children use counting strategies and typically model the activity directly by using objects or fingers. Later they develop rather complicated counting strategies (Baroody, 2004).

Most preschoolers have developed a counting schema for the numbers 1–5, a quantity schema that allows them to think of small quantities in comparison to one another, and they can use words to talk about changes that can be made. However, they do not connect the ideas until later. (Starkey, 1992; Siegler & Robinson, 1982; Gelman, 1978).

Young children can think about small numbers without having the physical objects (Steffe & Cobb, 1988).

Children often do not understand mathematical words in a problem situation and require modeling with concrete objects and words to develop an "operation sense" (Copley & Hawkins, 2005).

The Teacher's Role in Promoting Understanding of Number and Operations

Although young children naturally begin to develop some informal mathematical understandings, many more opportunities to learn more school-based or formal mathematics need to be provided. The teacher's role is critical to that development. Generally, teachers should identify everyday situations that involve numbers and operations and intentionally teach those concepts to children through daily routines, choice-time activities, and large- and small-group instruction. Many teaching strategies contribute to children's development of numerical understanding.

Practice counting, using a variety of learning styles and representations. Count, using rhymes and verses and in ways that involve children physically. For example, children can touch their heads, shoulders, waists, knees, and toes as they count so that they can practice one-to-one correspondence. On occasion, point to the numerals on a chart as children count aloud. The numerals have a visual pattern, and the auditory and visual clues used together are helpful.

Provide a variety of materials to help children develop an understanding of quantity. Introduce children to many different number representations, for example, pips on a domino or number cube, tally marks, footsteps, fingers, counters of all kinds, and a wide variety of art materials. Ask them to create sets of two, three, four, or five using concrete materials. After they have created many concrete sets, children can draw pictures or paste cutouts on paper to represent specific quantities.

Model counting strategies. Model correct counting. As you count, demonstrate how to keep track of objects you have counted and announce one number to tell *how many* are in a set. Label what you counted (e.g., five boys or three fingers) and record the answer using numerals and words.

Model comparing the number of objects in two sets. Compare two lines of children by having them join hands with a partner in the other line. Then emphasize that the people who do not have a partner are in the line with *more* people and the people who have a partner are in the line with *fewer* or *less* people. Do the same task with objects showing how the objects are individually matched to compare.

Identify everyday situations in which to use ordinal numbers. As children participate in routine activities such as taking turns to wash hands, working in interest areas, or listening to their favorite stories, use ordinal numbers to describe people or objects. For example, you could say, "The first person to run the obstacle course is Dallas," or "I think the second block in your tower is the biggest one," or "The third goat had the hardest time getting over the bridge." You can also play hiding games in which you hide a particular object under one of four cups. A child must figure out whether the object is under the first, second, third, or fourth cup. Emphasizing the words for ordinal numbers is critical to children's understanding.

Make obvious mistakes so that children can identify the errors. Using a favorite puppet, pretend to count incorrectly, forget number names, mix up terms like *more* and *fewer*, and give wrong answers. Encourage children to correct the puppet and respond correctly. After the children are secure in their number understanding, you can make mistakes as well; however, make them very obvious and talk aloud to indicate that you might make a mistake. "I can't remember..." and "I wonder what comes next..." are two good beginning phrases.

Illustrate and model a variety of problems that involve combining, separating, sharing, or set-making. Use everyday situations to model the use of operations. Helpers can pass out materials so everyone gets the same amount, class treats can be shared, and the total number of children in the class or an interest area can be constantly changed as children leave or enter during the school year.

Act out operation stories. Pose story problems that involve adding, subtracting, multiplying, or dividing. Have the children act out the stories, themselves or with objects. Then count to solve the problems. Use the numbers 1–5 and remember to emphasize the vocabulary that indicates the actions (e.g., *take away*).

Use books to encourage numerical reasoning. Many books that you share with your class include number questions or problems. After reading a book several times, add numbers to some of the sentences. Write the numbers on an adhesive note and put it on the page. Ask the children to tell *how many* or to solve a problem created with the numbers.

Encourage children to tell stories about *how many*. Ask children questions that prompt them to tell *how many*. For example, they can tell how many rode in the car during outdoor time, how many played at the water table, how many footsteps it took to walk across the room, or how many cookies they had after their friend gave them more.

Publish number books. Share a variety of number books. Cover some pages and then ask the children to tell which pages are missing. Help them create the missing pages. Have children write, illustrate, and publish class number books. Some possible titles for these books could be *All the Animals We Saw at the Zoo* or *The Purple Things We Found at School* or *The Eyes in Our Class*.

Create a numerically rich environment. Include numerals in every area of your classroom. Display them in written or cutout forms and include them as manipulatives where appropriate (e.g., magnetic numerals in the Toys and Games area, stamps in the Library area, sponges in the Art area). Include a variety of collections for counting and sorting activities. Number books as well as number stories should be included in the Library area. A calendar, attendance chart, lunch or snack numbers, and any other management tool with numbers should be displayed. Counters of every kind should be easily available as well as number lines, a hundred chart, and a clearly written list of numerals (*1–20*). Props that include numbers for the Dramatic Play area should be prominently displayed so students can use them as they play (e.g., grocery receipts, old checkbooks, price lists). Games that include dice and require children to move spaces also contribute to children's counting skills.

Assessing Children's Progress

To assess children's progress with number and operations, observe children consistently and regularly. Observe children in interest areas and in group settings as they

- count sets of objects
- solve number problems
- play games that require them to move one, two, or three spaces
- compare the number of items in two sets of objects
- "see" small groups of numbers
- write symbols for quantities

As children complete activities or work in small groups, ask the following questions:

How many are there? How did you find out?

Which set has more? How do you know?

How many do you see? Why do you think so?

I have three counters. John gives me two more. How many do I have now?

Jeffrey has four cookies. The dog ate two of them. How many cookies does Jeffrey have left?

Amy's mom made 30 cookies. Do we have enough for everyone to get two cookies?

How far can you count? What number comes before 10? After 30?

Why are you adding one more spoon to that place?

How many balloons do you think we should have for the party? Why do you think so?

Tips to Share With Families

- Count everything! Touch the objects as you say the corresponding numbers.

- Count incorrectly or lose track of which objects you have already counted. Encourage children to help you find your errors.

- Read counting books with your child frequently. Together, check each page to see whether the number of pictured objects matches the numeral on the page. After the objects on a page are counted, hide some of them with a small piece of paper or your hand. Ask children to decide how many objects are hidden.

- Ask children to help set the table, distributing the same number of each object to each place, or ask them to tell how many more they need of something to have a particular number.

- Concentrate on either the number 5 or 10. Ask children to use their fingers to talk about parts of 5 (2 fingers on one hand and 3 fingers on the other hand, or 1 finger on one hand and 4 fingers on the other). In a similar manner, ask children to talk about the parts of 10 (for example, 3 fingers have rings and 7 fingers do not, or 2 thumbs and 8 other fingers).

- Play games with 5 objects and 10 objects. For example, suggest that children toss 5 or 10 pennies, or 5 or 10 puffballs. They should count and tell how many pennies land "heads-up" and how many land "heads-down." They can identify how many puffballs land in a plastic cup target and how many land outside of the cup.

Geometry and Spatial Sense

Young children find geometry an exciting topic. Unfortunately, many early childhood teachers only focus children's attention on learning about four shapes: square, rectangle, triangle, and circle. There is so much more to investigate! In preschool, there are four important geometry concepts young children need to explore and understand.

Shape

Both two- and three-dimensional shapes are important to the understanding of geometry. Young children need to recognize shapes, build with them, illustrate them in their own way, describe shapes' attributes, compare shapes, and sort them by their characteristics. Naming shapes is not the most important aspect of this topic. However, children should be exposed to the correct geometric terms for shapes, and they should be given opportunities to identify shapes by both name and what they look like. (See the Glossary.) Finally, young children should be encouraged to predict what will happen when they build and create with shapes or put together two- or three-dimensional shapes.

Some three-dimensional shapes that preschool children can easily identify include

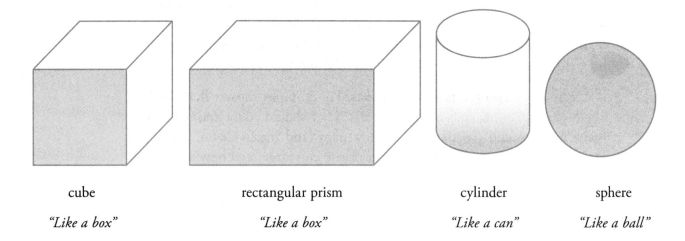

cube	rectangular prism	cylinder	sphere
"Like a box"	*"Like a box"*	*"Like a can"*	*"Like a ball"*

Space

Children should describe shapes and other objects using relationship words like *near, under, by, on top of, right,* and *left.* They should be able to locate and find shapes or other objects when given simple verbal directions or when using maps with pictures and diagrams. Shapes should be positioned in a variety of ways and orientations in space so that children can identify them regardless of how they are positioned.

Transformations

Moving shapes by sliding them to a new position, flipping them over, turning, or combining them are important geometric skills. Notice how children use these skills when they work puzzles, attempt to fit blocks on a shelf, or mold clay to make a model of a three-dimensional shape. Young children also can create shapes that are symmetrical, as shown in the following illustration.

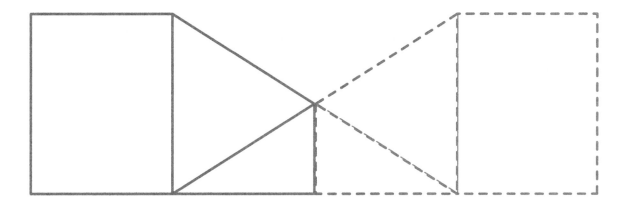

Visualization

Young children should be able to picture geometric shapes mentally after seeing them and then represent what they visualized by using the same geometric shapes or drawings. Also give children opportunities to see pictures or drawings from different orientations (e.g., portrait or landscape) and block creations from different perspectives, (e.g., from the top, side, and underneath).

What Does Research Say?

Children do not develop their ideas about shapes from simply looking at them. They must manipulate, draw, or represent the shapes in a variety of ways (Clements, 1999).

Three- and 4-year-old children typically recognize shapes in a variety of orientations. As children get older, they identify particular shapes only if they are in one orientation. That is, a triangle is a triangle only if it is "flat on a side" (Copley, 2000).

Typically, young children judge shapes by appearance as a whole; that is, a triangle is a triangle because it "looks like one" (Van Hiele, 1986).

Children learn about shapes during their preschool years, and their understandings about shape stabilize as early as age 6 (Clements, 1999).

Three-year-olds can build simple, yet meaningful maps with landscape toys such as houses, cars, and trees. Older preschoolers can learn the relative distances between landmarks (Clements, 2000).

With experience, preschool children can develop visualization. They can observe a shape picture using five shapes, remember it by visualizing what they just saw, and then make the picture accurately using the appropriate shapes in the correct relationship to each other (Copley, 2004).

Four- and 5-year-old children can move shapes to determine whether they are identical to other shapes; they slide, rotate, and sometimes flip the shapes to determine whether they match (Clements, 2003).

Children in an environment where they investigated shapes by combining, folding, cutting, drawing, and copying them were able to select examples of specific shapes much more accurately than children who had not been provided the rich, investigative environment (Clements, 1999).

Visualization and spatial reasoning are improved with interaction with computer animations and in other technological settings (Clements et al., 1997).

The Teacher's Role in Promoting Understanding of Geometry

Geometry is a topic that young children naturally explore and enjoy. They build amazing constructions with blocks, create pictures with shapes, and view objects from a variety of perspectives as a result of their constant movement. The teacher's role is to encourage children to reflect on these activities, to use appropriate vocabulary to describe shapes or the orientation of objects, to scaffold children's understanding as they explore, and to encourage children who are not playing with geometry to investigate the ideas. Specific teaching strategies can be used to support young learners of geometry.

Provide opportunities for all children to use the Block area. The Block area is the perfect place for children to explore the attributes of three-dimensional shapes. For example, when children stack blocks, they naturally investigate the surface to see whether it is flat and can stack easily or whether it is curved and cannot stack. All children should have access to this important area, including children with disabilities.

Label shapes with correct names as the children use them. Use the correct names for shapes. This can be done by simply adding vocabulary to the child's descriptions or manipulations. For example, when a child says, "I got a round one," when describing a sphere, you can say, "Yes, it is round. It looks like a ball. I call it a *sphere*." When a child identifies a square correctly, you can say, "Yes, it is a square. I call it a *square-rectangle*, because it is a special kind of rectangle." Refer to the appendix of this volume for a list of common two- and three-dimensional shapes and their descriptions.

Provide a rich variety of shapes for investigation. Unit blocks are essential for teaching and learning geometric concepts. A variety of other three-dimensional shapes are important as well. Hemispheres, triangular prisms, triangular pyramids, rectangular prisms, square pyramids, and spheres provide many other contrasting experiences for children. The same is true for two-dimensional shapes. Often children are only introduced to shapes that have sides of equal lengths. To develop a real understanding of shape, children need to see *squashed* triangles, *really long* rectangles, *funny-shaped* pentagons, and other shapes with unusual configurations.

Ask children to predict and investigate what will happen when two shapes are combined. Introduce activities that require children to match sides or surfaces of two shapes. Asking children to make a tall, smooth tower out of unit blocks encourages them to predict and then investigate how to accomplish that task. Similarly, giving children a set of identical right triangles and asking them to match sides to create shapes encourages a discovery of new squares, triangles, or quadrilaterals.

Shapes Made From Two Congruent Triangles

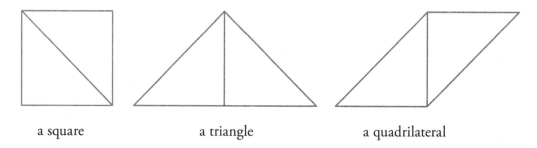

a square   a triangle   a quadrilateral

Model and describe how to make two- and three-dimensional shapes.

Create a particular shape using clay, paper, or another flexible material and describe it as you work. For example, as you transform a clay ball unto a cylinder, you can say, "I am rolling the clay to make the sides smooth. Now I am patting it on the ends so that it will have flat circles on the top and bottom." As you cut paper to make a triangle, you might say, "I need to cut off this corner so I have a straight side. Now I need two more straight sides to make a triangle."

Guide children to act out stories that use positional and spatial words.

Many familiar stories use positional words to describe the motions of a character or an object. *The Three Billy Goats Gruff* and *Goldilocks and the Three Bears* are just two favorites that provide opportunities for children to explore concepts such as *near, inside, outside, far, under, over, next to, between,* and *on top of.*

Begin with three-dimensional shapes.

Children need to hold and manipulate objects before they work with paper representations of objects. The same is true as children explore geometric shapes. Building with three-dimensional shapes, rolling them down ramps, tossing them at targets, and modeling three-dimensional shapes with clay are all good beginning activities for children. Three-dimensional shapes should be used to introduce the two-dimensional shapes, for example, by making block prints in water, paint, or clay. The resulting prints can then be identified as the more common two-dimensional shapes (e.g., a cube makes six square prints, a square pyramid makes four triangle prints and one square print.)

Provide activities that ask children to visualize and represent particular shapes.
Show children photos, models, or sketches of particular shapes or combinations of shapes. Ask children to look and remember what they have seen; then hide the representation. Have children recreate the photo, model, or sketch by using their own shapes. As children develop this skill and have more frequent practice, the models and shape orientations can become more complex and more difficult to visualize and remember.

Use technology to help children visualize geometric ideas. Computer technology allows children to manipulate shapes and visualize the results quickly and frequently. Often, preschool children's less-developed fine-motor skills make it difficult for them to move particular blocks so that the others remain in place. Computer technology allows children easily to make the movements piece by piece, see errors, and then correct their actions.

Use the word not to introduce non-examples of specific shapes. To fully understand the attributes of particular shapes, it is critical that young children know what shapes are *not* classified as a particular shape. Create many opportunities for children to sort shapes into two groups, those that are the shape and those that are *not* the shape.

Make class maps and have children use them to find particular objects. Children love a mystery! Hide or select a particular classroom object. Give the children a map of the classroom with identifiable landmarks and specific clues about the object's location. Have the children search for the hidden object by using the map. For example, if the object is hidden *under* a box-like wastebasket, there could be a sketch of a rectangular prism with an arrow indicating *under*. With older preschoolers, try giving clues that involve relative distances, that is, clues that tell how far an object is from a landmark.

Suggest that children sketch their building plans so that they can be remembered.
Encourage children to represent their constructions in a variety of ways. They can create sketches or blueprints using black crayons on white or blue rolled paper or on newsprint. Take photos of the buildings and attach them to the representation. Do not forget to have the builders sign the representation. Then place it in the Block area for future architects and builders to use.

Encourage the discovery of shape attributes. Rather than telling children about a shape's attributes, plan experiences that allow them to experiment with shapes and discover them on their own. Ramps allow children to discover which three-dimensional shapes roll, slide, and stand; targets invite them to toss shapes; and feely bags allow children to discover the attributes through touch. Cutting and folding, collage, and printing activities are all vehicles for exploring the attributes of two-dimensional shapes. The discoveries children make on their own are much more important than anything you can tell them. You guide and extend learning when you label their discoveries by using their words and incorporating geometric terminology.

As children work puzzles, use words like turn, flip, or slide to explain how the pieces might fit. Transformational language for young children includes the words *turn*, *flip*, and *slide*. As teachers interact with children who are working puzzles, they can teach transformational words by stating how a child should manipulate a puzzle piece, by describing what the child does—turn, flip, or slide—or by helping to work a puzzle while describing their own movements. Both commercial and teacher-made puzzles can be used to help young children learn to transform shapes from one orientation to another. Teachers can also create other opportunities for children to fit shapes together by having them fill in a quilt square or a particular size piece of paper so that there is no space showing.

Have children clean up by placing shapes on a shelf or in a box so they can easily fit. Opportunities for cleanup abound in an early childhood classroom. When shelves in the Block area are labeled as described in *The Creative Curriculum for Preschool, Volume 2: Interest Areas*, children can match the blocks with their two-dimensional representations. In the Toys and Games area, containers can be labeled so that children can place all the triangles together, all the circles together, or all the squares together.

Assessing Children's Progress

To assess children's progress with geometry, observe students regularly. Observe children in interest areas and in other group settings as they

- manipulate shapes
- create structures or make pictures by using shapes
- name or label shapes during class activities and in their environments
- experiment with shape attributes
- describe the attributes of shapes
- work puzzles
- use geometric vocabulary appropriately
- work in the Block area
- move shapes to fit into a confined space

As children complete activities or work in small groups, ask the following questions about shapes:

How is this shape like this one? How is it different?

What would happen if I moved this shape here?

Why isn't this shape a_____? Why is it called a _____?

What if I turned this shape? What would it look like if I flipped it? What would happen if I slid it from your paper to mine?

Where have you seen this shape before?

Can you make a picture out of shapes?

Do you think this would roll?.... slide?.... stack?

How could you cut this paper to make another shape?

What shape could you make out of these two shapes?

What would happen if I dropped this block and it broke?

What would happen if I cut off an end of this shape? What would it look like?

Can you make a square? A triangle? A rectangle with pipe cleaners? How about a ball? A box? Or a cone?

Ask questions related to spatial sense:

How can I get to the cafeteria from here? To the office from our classroom?

Tell me about the city you have made in the Block area. Pretend I cannot see it. What does it look like?

Tips to Share With Families

- Encourage children to build towers with blocks. Talk about the blocks that make the best towers and the specific shapes that do not work well.

- Help your child understand geometric vocabulary by using objects. For example, explain, *A cylinder is like a can. A sphere is like a ball, and a square is like the side of this box.*

- Invite children to make particular three-dimensional shapes (cubes, cylinders, or spheres) with play dough or clay.

- Take photos of block constructions that children have made. Ask them to rebuild the constructions by using the photo as a guide.

- Play "Look, Draw, and Fix." Draw a picture by using squares, circles, and triangles. Ask children to look at it. Then hide the picture and ask the children to draw it from memory. Then uncover yours and ask the children to fix their pictures if they do not match the one you drew.

- Encourage children to work puzzles. Use words like *turn, slide,* or *flip* to help them decide where to place their puzzle pieces.

Measurement

Measurement is an important, practical mathematical concept that you often hear children discussing with their peers:

I'm bigger than you!

Wow, that giraffe can really stretch his neck huge!

This rock is fat...I can't move it.

I'm four years old...I just had my birthday party!

As these few examples illustrate, children naturally use the language of measurement and comparison to discuss their surroundings and their relationships to other children. Although the language they use is often incorrect or general, they still love to compare objects using size as an attribute. Young children watch adults use measurement tools and use measurement to solve problems in their world. Children begin to model measurement behaviors and frequently experiment with both standard and nonstandard tools. There are three measurement topics that should be explored by preschool children.

Measurement Attributes

Young children are aware that there are different ways of describing measurements. They begin to recognize the attributes of *length* (how long or tall something is), *capacity* (how much something holds), *weight* (how heavy something is), *area* (how much space is covered), and *time*. However, they often are unable to use the correct vocabulary to describe a particular attribute. They frequently over-use the words *big* or *little* when describing length, volume, weight, area, and even time. Before children learn how to measure, they must first be able to describe and differentiate the attributes of an object by length, capacity, weight, and area.

Comparing and Ordering

Comparison is a fundamental concept that enables children fully to develop an understanding of measurement. They begin by comparing two objects by specific attributes: describing one object as being taller or shorter than the other, holding more or holding less than the other, being heavier or lighter than the other, or covering more or less space than the other. They also can describe an event as taking more or less time than another. Next, children compare three or more objects or events and place them in order. This is a much more difficult task and one that requires many problem-solving, experimental experiences.

Measurement Behaviors and Processes

Actual measurement involves assigning a number to an attribute of an object, such as the length of a crayon or the capacity of a jar. Understanding how to measure accurately is a skill that takes many years to learn. The process of measuring is based on three fundamental concepts:

- conservation—a set maintains the same quantity no matter how its parts are arranged or rearranged; an object maintains the same length if it is bent; an amount of liquid poured from one container into a differently sized container retains the same quantity

- transitivity—if length A is less than length B, and length B is less than length C, then length A is less than length C

- unit—the number and size of units is used consistently for the measurement of one object

To learn these three concepts, young children first experiment with nonstandard measuring tools (e.g., straws or yarn to measure their height, rice or sand in plastic tubs to measure how much "cookie dough" they need for their party, and rocks or marbles to measure the weight of the class gerbil). Experimenting with nonstandard units is a preliminary step to understanding why the use of standard tools is important for accurate measurement. In preschool, experimentation with measurement behaviors is essential to mathematical understanding. Children will learn how to *conserve*, to reason with *transitivity*, to select appropriate *units* or tools for the attribute being measured, and measure with multiple copies of units of the same size (e.g., using teddy bears laid end to end to measure the length of a classroom rug).

What Does Research Say?

Young children know that attributes of length, weight, capacity, and time exist, but they do not know how to reason about them or measure them accurately (Clements, 2003).

Preschool children are interested in measuring and begin to develop understandings about important measurement concepts during the ages 3–5 (Clements, 2003).

Children's initial ideas about the size or quantity of an object are based on perception. They judge that one object is bigger than another because it looks bigger (Piaget & Inhelder, 1967).

Preschool children can learn significant ideas about measuring. They can arrange objects side by side to compare their lengths. They can hold one object in each hand to compare their weights if the weights are significantly different. They can lay one leaf on top of another to see which has the greater area if the smaller shape fits within the boundary of the larger leaf (Clements, 2003).

Four-year-old children can begin to learn the process of measuring with nonstandard units. They can lay identical plastic chains end to end across the length of a room and count the number of chains. They can cover a sheet of paper with sticky notes to measure the area of the sheet of paper. They can use teddy bear counters to measure the weight of a toy (Copley, 2004).

Current thinking and research suggests that children can benefit from using rulers along with concrete models of units, even during beginning activities with measurement (Clements, 2003).

The Teacher's Role in Promoting Understanding of Measurement

The goal of measurement activities in preschool is to encourage exploration, not mastery. Teachers should introduce measurement concepts through a variety of experiences while using the appropriate vocabulary to describe the process. Most importantly, teachers should not limit their expectations of young children when it comes to measurement. Providing a variety of experiences along with reflection and communication about those experiences will likely produce some surprising results. Here are important strategies:

Provide many standard measuring tools for children to use. While measuring with standard units is not emphasized at the preschool level, standard measuring tools should be a part of the classroom environment. Rulers, yardsticks, meter sticks, measuring tapes, balance scales, centimeter grid paper, and marked measuring cups are tools that should be accessible to children in the classroom. Children should be encouraged to use them as they want for their measuring experiences. Similarly, teachers and other adults should use them as intended during appropriate class activities.

Model measuring behaviors frequently. Many measurement opportunities occur throughout the day in preschool. Measuring the length of the Library area when you need a new rug, using a clock to judge how many more minutes you have until lunch, deciding whether a stack of books is too heavy to carry, or deciding whether a piece of butcher paper is big enough to cover a table are all measurement activities. To help children develop an understanding of measurement, these activities need to be modeled explicitly for children. Thinking aloud, or describing what you are doing, as you measure will likely prompt children to explore measurement on their own.

Talk about what you are doing as you measure. An important aspect of any modeling activity is the oral language that is used to describe the activity. Talk aloud as you model the measurement activity, to help children focus on the activity and the particular measurement strategy that is being used.

Encourage measurement problem-solving activities. Many problem-solving activities also involve measurement. Toy car races between the teacher's car and the class's car provide good opportunities to explore *measuring fairly,* especially when the distance the teacher's car travels is measured with tiny sticks and the distance the class's car travels is measured with long sticks. Having children completely cover a paper quilt with different rectangular shapes requires them to experiment with area. Making a straw bridge for the *Three Billy Goats Gruff* creates an opportunity for understanding the concept of weight. Preparing cookies for the entire class requires measuring capacity, counting, and addition operations.

Take advantage of daily experiences to discuss measurement concepts. Many daily experiences lead to discussions about measurement concepts, particularly time. Almost every day, children ask and teachers answer questions like these: "How much choice time is left?…How much longer until outdoor time?…When is snack time?…Is it time for clean-up?" They are also perfect opportunities to introduce a timer. Using a timer allows children to see time passing and, when used along with comparative words to describe the time, children begin to develop an understanding of time measurement.

Use estimation vocabulary. Many measurements do not need to be exact. Often, only rough estimates are required for length, weight, or capacity measures. Children need to hear estimation vocabulary such as *about*, *close to*, and *almost* in the context of real-life situations.

Assessing Children's Progress

To assess children's progress with measurement, observe students consistently and regularly. Observe children in interest areas and in group settings as they

- use measuring tools
- try to fit objects into particular spaces
- compare the size of objects
- use measurement vocabulary
- pour water or rice into containers
- use the term *bigger* to describe something

As children complete activities or work in small-group settings, ask the following questions:

About length

Which one is longer? Shorter?

Can you find something that is longer than this? Shorter? Can you show me?

How much ribbon will you need to go around this? Can you figure it out just by looking?

Can you put these three straws in order from the shortest to the longest? How can you show me that your answer is right? Where would you put the fourth straw? How did you know?

About area

Which shape can be covered with the most blocks? The least?

Will it take more blocks to cover the table or the book? How can you show that your answer is right?

What if you used cubes to cover the book? Would it take more cubes or more blocks to cover it?

About weight

Which is heavier? Lighter? How do you know?

How can you show which person weighs more? Less?

Put these three rocks on the balance, one at a time. How can you tell which rock is the heaviest? The lightest?

About capacity

Which container holds the most? The least? Why do you think so?

How can you find out which container holds the most water?

Suppose you had three containers. How would you find out which one holds the most water if you could only fill one container at a time?

About time

Will it take longer to walk to the door or to write your name?

Will it take longer than a minute to walk home? Why do you think so?

What do we do when we come to school? What do we do after that? Before lunch?

What do we spend the most time doing in our class?

Tips to Share With Families

- Use measurement vocabulary and talk aloud as you make common measurements around the house, in the store, or while traveling. For example, you might explain,

  It should take about 20 minutes to get to the store. It is about 15 miles from home, and we can travel on the highway.

  I need three cups of flour for the cake. I will need to buy enough at the grocery store.

  We need to buy a tablecloth for the kitchen table. I think we should buy one that is about 5 square feet.

- Invite children to estimate how many cups will fill the bowl, how far it is from their bedroom door to the front door, how long it will take to finish cleaning up their toys, how many tiles it will take to cover the entryway, how heavy the book bag is, or how tall they will be a year from now.

- Model the measuring you do in a typical day. Talk aloud as you model the use of a variety of measuring tools when you cook, make household repairs, drive, build, sew, and so on.

Patterns (Algebra)

Algebraic concepts are key to a good basic understanding of mathematics. The recognition, creation, and extension of patterns and the analysis of change are important pre-algebraic concepts for preschool children. The study of patterns and change are exciting topics for young children and can be a strong motivation for discovery and creative thinking.

Patterns

Children begin to identify patterns at an early age. A consistent daily schedule, the phrases in a song or verse, or the repeated colors of the wall tiles are all patterns that can be easily recognized and described by young children. Extending those patterns in a consistent way is a skill that can be taught to young children and, with practice, transferred from one representation to another. Patterns in sequences of sounds and movement (e.g., stomp, clap, clap; stomp, clap, clap; stomp, clap, clap...), colors in a striped shirt (e.g., blue, red; blue, red; blue, red...) and shapes and positions in a block wall (e.g., block up, down; up, down; up, down...) are examples of repeating patterns

because each unit is repeated in a consistent way. To translate one pattern representation to another, a child must be able to read the pattern using her own words and then read it another way. For example, the cylinder block pattern shown above could be read, "block like a can standing tall, block like a can on its side; block like a can standing tall, block like a can on its side." Then it could be translated to the sound pattern of "stomp, clap; stomp, clap; stomp, clap."

Growing patterns are also important as children's algebraic thinking matures. They become critical to children's understanding of number operations. The plus-one pattern is a growing number pattern because one is added to each number and therefore increases by one each term of the pattern. The following picture of a block staircase is an example of a plus-one pattern.

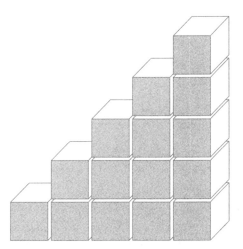

Many rhymes and songs used in early childhood classrooms are examples of growing patterns. In the familiar song "My Aunt Came Back," children add one phrase and action to each verse until they reach the tenth verse with ten actions and phrases. The song is a perfect example of a growing pattern—and one that is fun to perform!

Change

Young children love to talk about how they have grown or how tall they are. Analyzing change is an important algebraic concept and one that can begin at a young age. To analyze change, children can talk about it qualitatively:

I am bigger than my brother 'cause I growed!

When I was little, I drank milk from a bottle. Now that I am big, I drink from a glass.

Our eggs have hatched! Look at the chickens!

Children can also describe quantitative change by using numbers. The growth of the pet gerbil, the change in the height of a bean plant, or the change from one day to the next in the number of children who drink milk are all examples of quantitative change to which young children can relate.

What Does Research Say?

Very young children are interested in patterns and can learn to copy simple patterns made with objects. Subsequently, they can learn to extend and create their own patterns (Clements, 2004).

Young children can determine the unit of a repeating pattern and can use this skill to determine that two perceptually different patterns actually have the same structure (e.g., red, blue; red, blue; red, blue and stomp, clap; stomp, clap; stomp, clap) (Clements, 2004).

Children will often identify an incomplete unit to repeat or grow. They do not see the part or unit that is being repeated or growing as a whole (Copley, 2005).

Before age 5, children can learn to copy simple patterns made with objects and subsequently learn to extend patterns and create their own patterns (Clements, 2003).

Children often believe that something is a pattern simply because a color or shape is repeated once. They do not see that it must be repeated or grow many times before a pattern is established (Copley, 2005).

From the earliest age, children can be learning the basic rudiments of algebra, particularly its representational aspects. When both patterns and their representations are emphasized, the basic ideas of algebra are introduced (Kilpatrick, Swafford, & Findell, 2001).

As young children extend patterns, they are making conjectures that are logical and make sense from their perspective (Carpenter & Levi, 1999).

The Teacher's Role in Developing Understanding of Patterns

Many young children naturally search for patterns, but their discoveries need to be labeled and extended. The teacher's role is to challenge children to identify patterns in many settings, represent those patterns auditorily and with objects, and extend those patterns in consistent ways. In addition, the teacher should provide many opportunities for children to create their own patterns with objects, sounds, or words and purposefully teach children different representations for the patterns they identify. Teachers also need to guide children to analyze the changes that occur in their everyday lives by asking them to use words or numbers to talk about the changes they observe. Several particular teaching strategies can contribute to children's understanding of algebraic concepts.

Identify different patterns in daily routines. Job assignments, the class schedule, and other daily procedures can be identified and labeled as patterns. If outdoor time is always after snack, the pattern can be written on colored paper and identified as a class pattern (e.g., on Monday, snack [red paper], outdoors [blue paper]; on Tuesday, snack [red paper], outdoors [blue paper]; on Wednesday, snack [red paper], outdoors [blue paper]; and so on.) In any preschool classroom, patterns in daily routines abound. Teachers should consistently help children identify them.

Encourage pattern "talk" and identification. "Look, it's a pattern!" should be a common expression in a preschool classroom. Initially, teachers model patterns and "think out loud" when seeing patterns (e.g., "Let's walk like an elephant, swaying back and forth and moving our trunks: right, left; right, left; right, left. Oh, it's a pattern!" "Jonathan, you have a pattern on your shirt: blue stripe, red stripe; blue stripe, red stripe."). As children become pattern "detectives," encourage them to describe the patterns they identify and represent them (e.g., in a class book titled, *Patterns Discovered by Our Class*).

Point to numerals as you count out loud. Rote counting is a familiar pattern. The numerical sequence of one, two, three, four, five, six, seven, eight, and nine repeats as children count higher and higher. Because some of the words used to name numbers are unusual (e.g., *eleven* rather than *ten-one* or *twelve* rather than *ten-two* or *fifteen* rather than *ten-five*), the auditory patterns are not as obvious as the visual patterns. The numerals *11, 12, 13, 14,* and *15* have an easily recognizable visual pattern and, if pointed out, can be identified by children.

Begin with color patterns and progress to shape and size patterns. Color patterns are the easiest patterns for young children to identify. Help children create patterns by isolating one attribute at a time. For example, encourage children to use objects that are identical except for color to help them create color patterns. Next, have them use objects that are the same color but different shapes. Continue the sequence with same-colored, same-shaped, and differently sized objects.

Describe positional patterns. Positional patterns are not the typical patterns described in preschool classrooms. However, they provide a good opportunity to take spatial terms that are critical to geometric understanding and connect them to algebraic ideas. Block or object patterns can be described with words like *up, down, right, left, high, low, crooked,* or *straight.* To encourage the use of positional patterns, provide children with identical blocks or objects. This will help them focus on the attribute of position rather than color, shape, or size.

Focus on the unit that is to be repeated in a pattern. To help children focus on the pattern unit, children can "become" part of the unit. For example, to make sidewalk chalk patterns, one child can use the green chalk to make a squiggly line, another child can use the pink chalk to make a squiggly line, and still another child can use the pink chalk to make a squiggly line. The pattern unit—green squiggly, pink squiggly, pink squiggly—would be emphasized, because each child would need to take a turn in order to make the pattern. The pattern unit could then be recorded on a piece of black paper to emphasize the repetition of the unit written on the sidewalk.

Use patterned stories and verses. Many stories and verses repeat events or phrases in a patterned, consistent manner. These patterns can be illustrated and extended by writing additional parts for the verses or stories. *Mrs. McTats and Her Houseful of Cats* (Alyssa S. Capucilli), *The Napping House* (Audrey Wood), and *The Relatives Came* (Cynthia Rylant) are books that include patterns that can be acted out easily by children. This is a wonderful way to connect mathematics and literacy.

Create pattern and change books. Encourage children to represent patterns they have discovered or created by making books with illustrations of the patterns. Photos of patterns combined with children's illustrations of the same patterns provide children with both two-dimensional, real representations and more abstract representations. Similarly, class stories that represent change can be illustrated with children's drawings or photos. Books such as *When I Was Little: A Four-Year-Old's Memoir of Her Youth* (Jamie Lee Curtis) can be used as models for children's creations. Children can complete phrases like, "When I was little, I could…. Now that I am big, I can…."

Provide opportunities to observe change. By including plants and animals in the classroom, children are presented with natural opportunities to observe change. They also have a chance to learn that change does not always occur in predictable ways, for example, as indicated by the rapid expansion of the class gerbil population. As changes occur, teachers should describe them by using both words and numbers (e.g., "We had just two gerbils, and now we have lots!" "In our gerbil cage, we had 2 gerbils. Then we had 8, and now we have 17!")

Use a variety of representations for patterns. Patterns should be described with sounds, words, movements, and objects rather than letters (e.g., red, blue; red, blue; red, blue rather than a, b; a, b; a, b). Because children are learning letters and the sounds each represent, the use of letters to represent patterns can be confusing and should be avoided.

Extend pattern units for at least five units in order to establish a pattern. A pattern is a pattern *only if* it consistently repeats or grows. A pattern cannot be established if a unit is only used one or two times. To encourage children to recognize and extend patterns, they must first be introduced to well-established patterns.

Assessing Children's Progress

To assess children's progress with algebraic understanding, observe children consistently and regularly. Observe children in interest areas, during transitions, and in group settings as they

- create patterns by using objects
- identify patterns in their environment
- follow movement patterns
- notice patterns in stories or verses
- can begin to use more complex patterns
- add to patterns created or discovered by other students
- predict what will happen next in the class schedule
- suggest unusual patterns
- use words to describe patterns or changes
- observe changes in classmates, classroom animals, or classroom plants

As children complete activities or work in small-group settings, ask the following questions:

What do you think we should do next? What do we normally do after choice time? What happens after snack time?

Would blue or yellow be next? Why do you think so? What if it were green instead?

Oh, I ripped my new striped sweater! What color of yarn should I get to fill in the tear?

What shape should go here to finish this quilt? Would that fit the pattern? How?

How does your block wall look like the playground gate in this photo?

Can you read your pattern? Can you read it a different way? What if you started here? How would your pattern be different?

What if I hid part of your pattern? Could you figure out what part is missing?

What movements do you want us to make today during dance time? What patterns do you want us to follow?

Should this go next...or this? Why?

Let's go on a pattern trip around the school. What patterns do you see? Why should we take a picture of that pattern? How would you use words to describe the pattern?

What will happen on the next page of this story? Why do you think so? What pattern do you see in the story?

How did you change from the beginning of the year to the end of the year? How have you grown? What can you do now that you couldn't do when you began school?

Tips to Share With Families

- Identify patterns everywhere:

  clothing—plaids or repeated stripes, colors, and shapes

  tiles—repeated or growing squares in the kitchen, bathroom, or hall

  books—repeated or growing patterns on the cover or pages; repeated words or phrases

  behavior—repetitions in daily routines; clothing worn in various types of weather; walking, exercise, dance, or marching patterns.

- Encourage children to create and extend patterns with blocks or other toys. After they make a pattern, ask them to describe it (for example, a child could make a pattern of colored blocks and describe it as "Orange, blue; orange, blue; orange, blue; etc." A staircase growing pattern can be described as "One block, two blocks, three blocks, four blocks," and so on or as "One block, one more, one more, one more," and so on.

- Algebra includes the concept of change. Create books with your child about how much he or she has grown. A variety of titles can be used, for example, *I Was Two, but Now I Am Three* or *I Used to Be a Baby, but Now I Am Big!*

Data Analysis

Many preschool classrooms contain teacher-made graphs and pictures of data collected by children. An apple graph showing "Our Favorite Apples," pictures of "Things That Are Red," or a chart containing pictures of classroom activities and labeled "Our Schedule" are often posted on the walls around the classroom. These are important tools for data analysis and, if used appropriately, can facilitate children's mathematical understanding. Three important ideas that involve concepts of data analysis for preschool children are discussed below.

Sorting and Classifying

Using the attributes of objects to sort and classify is an important skill for young children in many content areas. Initially, children sort objects by separating a group of objects from a larger collection. Their sorting rule is often based on an arbitrary attribute such as "I like this one" or "These are my favorites." With more practice, children begin sorting more consistently, using one attribute to describe the objects in a set. They may label objects as *red* or *big* or *balls* and place all objects that have that attribute to one side. Typically, children begin sorting by color, then by size, and then by shape. Other attributes, such as texture, sound, and function, are also used as sorting rules by young children but often inconsistently. After the objects are sorted and classified, the data needs to be organized so it can be represented and communicated to others.

Representing Data

In preschool classrooms, data is normally represented by using concrete objects, pictures, and graphs. The goal of graphing with young children is to provide a way of showing data about a child or his surroundings so it can be seen and understood. If displayed and labeled properly, children can make comparisons and describe what they see. Young children can often "become" the data in graphs, for example, by standing in a line with others who "like cheese crackers" or by sitting next to a classmate who "drinks chocolate milk." Afterwards, children can draw pictures to represent their preferences and place them in a bar graph or inside a circle to represent the organized data. Samples of data representation follow:

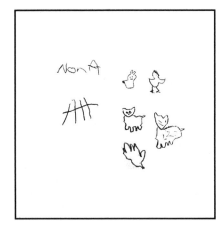
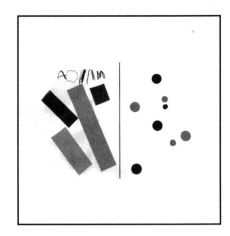

Describing Data

Vocabulary like *more*, *fewer*, the *same number as*, *larger than*, *smaller than*, and *not* can be used to describe data displayed on a graph or picture. These terms help connect the topic of number with data analysis. To describe data, it is important that young children separate sets of objects into two groups: one group that has a particular attribute and another group that does not have the attribute. Children who can describe and identify objects that are not red or not circles demonstrate an ability to describe data.

What Does Research Say?

Initially, children sort before they count the number of items in each group (Clements, 2003).

Children sort objects into groups before they can describe them with a label (Russell, 1991).

Typically, young children can only sort a set of objects by one attribute. Normally, it is difficult for 4- and 5-year-olds to classify a set of objects in more than one way (Copley, 2003).

The normal developmental progression of graphic representation is concrete (i.e., using physical objects, like toys, to make the graphs) to pictorial (i.e., using pictures of objects or drawings of toys) to symbolic (i.e., using letters to represent the color of toys, like *b* for a blue car and *r* for a red car) (Friel, Curio, & Bright, 2001).

With a variety of experiences, young children can read the data displayed in pictures and graphs (Kilpatrick, Swafford, & Findell, 2001).

The Teacher's Role in Promoting an Understanding of Data Analysis

A rich variety of experiences, particularly those involving sorting and classifying, help children understand the concepts and skills that underlie data analysis. Experiences that help children pose questions, collect data, organize data, represent data, and describe data are all very important aspects of this topic.

Here are important strategies:

Use classroom routines to represent data. Attendance, bus riders, and snack choices are examples of data that are accumulated in a typical preschool classroom. These data can be shown graphically or pictorially and described and counted using children's own words. Picture and name cards can be placed in a column labeled "bus rider" or "apple juice." When the cards are placed one above another, they form a bar graph that shows the number of people who will be riding the bus home or drinking apple juice at snack time.

Encourage children to organize objects by using their own rules. Young children naturally sort objects. Observe them as they sort and encourage them to explain why things are in particular piles or groups. Use their words to label their graphs or pictures and model appropriate vocabulary to describe the data.

Purposely describe collections in more than one way. Work with small groups of children to organize collections of objects. Ask them to tell how they organized the objects. To give them experience with classifying objects in more than one way, facilitate a variety of descriptions and model how they can all be methods.

Ask children to line up in classification groups. Create three-dimensional graphs by asking children to form two lines: one line that has children with a particular attribute or preference and the other line with children who do not have that particular attribute or preference. For example, children in one line could have tie shoes, and children in the other line could *not* have tie shoes; children in one line could be wearing red clothes, and children in the other line could *not* be wearing red clothes.

Use two groups to organize data. Rather than sorting objects into many groups, use two groups to sort: one group for objects that have the attribute and the other group for objects that do *not* have the attribute. This method enables children to classify objects easily and gives them an opportunity to understand the word *not*. For example, a can rolls when it is placed on its side on a ramp. It would fall into the category of objects that *roll*. A rectangular box will not roll no matter how it is placed on a ramp, so it would be classified as an object that does *not roll*.

Use paper of the same size to create bar graphs. Give each child paper of the same size and have each draw a picture of his or her snack or toy preference. When they are finished drawing, place each piece of paper in line, one above the other, to create bars for a graph (e.g., all the apples in one column, all the bananas in another column). Because the bars are made of paper of the same size, children can easily make comparisons and describe the data pictured.

Demonstrate classification and ask children to "guess" the describing words. Select a set of objects and ask the children to observe as you separate them into two groups. Model the classification process, slowly and thoughtfully considering each object as you place it in a group. When the sorting is complete, ask the children to describe each group in their own words. Check each child's "guess" by seeing whether the objects fit his or her rule.

Use symbols to represent data. Label graphs or other representations, using symbols that are easily understood by children. Color words can be written with matching crayons; pictures can be drawn and labeled with words; *not* can be indicated by writing or drawing a picture of the attribute and then drawing a large *X* across it. In the following example, the things that are red would be placed on the left side, and things that are *not* red would be placed on the right side.

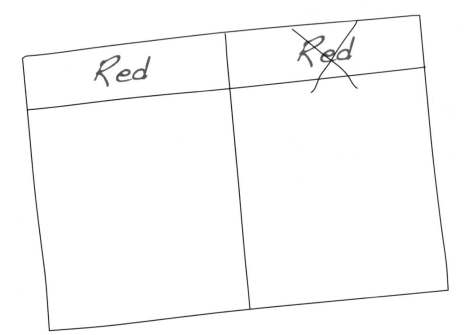

Assessing Children's Progress

To assess children's progress in understanding data analysis, observe children consistently and regularly. Observe children in interest areas and in group settings as they

- put objects in piles or groups
- talk about the class charts or graphs
- create art projects
- play classification games
- identify objects by color, size, or shape
- participate in class routines

As children complete activities or work in small groups, ask questions like these:

Which group has more? Which group has fewer?

How would you describe this group?

How are these two, three, four, or five objects alike? How are they different?

Why did you put that object here? Why did you put that object next to this one?

You said that these are all red. Can you find something that is not red?

Is there another name for these objects? Anything else?

Could this object go in your group? Why? Why not?

Tips to Share With Families

- Ask children to sort their toys, clothes, or shoes into two groups according to a common attribute like color (for example, red and not red), shape (for example, box and not box), or size (for example, big and not big) or according to another attribute (for example, laces or not laces, or stripes and not stripes). Decide which group has the most objects by matching an item from one group with an item from the other group.

- Make charts that show family job responsibilities, practice sessions, or homework assignments. Use checks or color coding to show when a job is complete.

- Invite children to put their drawings on a bulletin board or on the refrigerator in an organized way. Label the different sections (for example, *Jennifer's Pictures of Winter, Jennifer's Pictures of Our Family, Jennifer's Pictures of Our Dog*, and so on.)

- Make grocery lists together. Organize the items by groups (for example, cereals, dairy products, breads, meats, and so on).

- Make a photo album together. Label and organize the pictures as your child suggests.

- Organize a coin, stamp, or trading card collection.

- Help your child survey relatives or friends to find out what they like to eat, want for birthday presents, or wish. Report the findings to interested relatives or friends.

22

Mathematical Process Skills

Mathematical Process Skills

There is an air of excitement in *The Creative Curriculum* classroom where children are actively learning mathematics. Children in the Dramatic Play area sell flowers in the class "flower shop," **communicating** the prices of arrangements with handmade signs that say *20 pennies* or *lots of dollars*. In the Block area, children discuss blueprints or **representations** of earlier constructions, comparing them to attached photos. Nearby, two children discuss whether there will be enough cupcakes for everyone in the class to have two during an afternoon birthday celebration. They try to **solve the problem** by using a cupcake pan having spaces for a dozen cupcakes as well as the picture and word label for the pan. They wonder aloud as they begin to count, "How many will that make? Is that more cupcakes than children?"

In the Library area, three children **connect** what they have learned about patterns and books by creating a patterned border around each page of the class book, *Our Favorite Animals*. Finally, two children study a poster with a large circle in the middle. Some of the children's photos and names are *inside* the circle, while others are *outside* the circle. The children discuss why their pictures and names are inside the circle and explain their **reasoning**, "I'm in the circle 'cause I have glasses!" "No, I'm in the circle 'cause my name starts with *J* like *John* and *Jennifer*!"

The examples above illustrate five mathematical process skills identified by the National Council of Teachers of Mathematics as important for children's development and learning. These five process skills—**problem solving**, **reasoning**, **communicating**, **connecting**, and **representing**—are the means by which children learn the content described in chapter 21. They are an important part of mathematics instruction in *The Creative Curriculum* classroom and should be emphasized throughout the day. In this chapter, we describe each process skill, discuss how to teach and encourage skill development, and describe a routine example that focuses on that particular skill. While each process skill is discussed separately and individually, in reality they are neither separate nor inclusive of all processes, and they are part of each and every learning activity related to the components of mathematics.

Problem Solving

A problem is a question that prompts someone to find a solution, and young children love to solve problems! In fact, they spend much of their time solving problems that occur naturally in their everyday world. Some problems involve number; others are more geometric or spatial in nature. The questions young children pose often generate new mathematical questions or problems to solve. The teacher's role in the preschool classroom is to expand upon children's natural disposition to solve problems and ask new questions. Teachers also model an attitude of wonder and investigation.

Teaching and Encouraging Problem Solving

Problem solving is critical to helping children develop mathematical understandings. Through problem-solving experiences, children learn that there is a variety of ways to solve a problem and that a problem can have more than one answer or solution. Over time and with consistent nurturing, children develop into mature problem solvers. Here are important strategies for promoting children's problem solving skills:

Identify routine problem-solving opportunities. Problem-solving opportunities occur naturally during the day. For example, finding a place to store additional blocks in the Block area can be a geometric problem, determining whether there are enough snacks for the field trip is a number problem, deciding which of two rugs fits best in the large-group area is a measurement problem, and taking attendance and counting the children who are absent is a routine number activity that requires children to problem solve. These are just a few examples of how everyday situations present problem-solving opportunities. Teachers may overlook these opportunities or solve the problems, themselves. By doing so, they miss rich teaching and learning opportunities.

Use daily activities to teach problem solving. Problems also present themselves during daily activities, including story time. Books and stories are perfect contexts for problem solving. Characters can be added to a story, numerical situations can be improvised, mathematical vocabulary can be introduced, and story patterns can be extended. From these initial experiences, new stories or mathematical word problems can be created, acted out, and written. Other activities that occur during outdoor time and group times are perfect for teaching problem solving.

Use open-ended questions and comments. Of course, problem solving is encouraged when teachers ask questions and pose problems for children to solve. Questions like "Do we have enough?" or "What if there were 10 more apples?" prompt numerical solutions. Other questions, such as "What comes next in the pattern?" or "What shapes do you see in the block tower?" require word or pictorial solutions. Teachers' responses can further encourage problem solving. For example, if a teacher actively listens to children's solutions or responds to a possible solution with a neutral response, children continue to think and design solutions.

Model problem-solving behavior. The most important way a teacher can encourage problem solving is to model problem-solving behavior. They show a desire to solve problems, appear excited about solving problems, think aloud during the problem-solving process, and demonstrate the belief that children can solve problems in many ways.

A Routine Example of Problem Solving: "How Many Are Missing?"

During the spring, a playground situation led to a relevant problem-solving activity in one preschool classroom. Children were not responding to the teacher's signal that outdoor play was over and that it was time to return to the classroom. In fact, several children were often missing when the teacher was ready to lead them inside. She was continually solving the problem of how many were missing. Deciding that this would be a perfect time to enlist children's help, the teacher introduced the problem to children during their weekly theater time, which occurred each Friday. During theater time, the teacher usually read or told a story and invited some of the children to act out the events of the story while the others participated as the audience. Many of the stories were math-related stories that required children to find answers to particular problems. Children enjoyed acting out the stories, and they especially enjoyed the applause of their peers.

For the first "How Many Are Missing?" story, the teacher invited five children to act out a playground situation. When she signaled that it was time to return to the classroom, three children joined her while the others hid. The teacher asked the audience, "How many are missing?" The teacher invited several children to share their answers and their strategies for solving the problem. When the two missing children were revealed, the audience was delighted to see that they had indeed solved the problem. The children requested many more "How Many Are Missing?" stories during Friday theater time. Each story presented new subtraction problems for the children to solve.

The teacher then decided to teach problem-solving through other concrete experiences. She had children form pairs. Then she gave each pair a large piece of construction paper to represent the playground, a smaller piece of green paper to represent a bush, and counters to represent children. To begin, one child told a playground story by using the counters and then hid some of the counters under the bush. The other child listened to the story and then tried to solve the "How Many Are Missing?" problem. The storyteller lifted the bush to reveal the answer. The children reversed roles and new story problems were told and solved.

Problem-solving experiences often prompt other activities. In this instance, the class suggested making a book of "How Many Are Missing?" stories. Each child drew a playground scene with a chosen number of children. Then they attached a construction paper bush to hide some of the children and dictated their story problem to the teacher. The individual stories were combined to form a class book that was titled *How Many Are Missing?* and placed in the Library area. At choice time, the children could read a problem, solve it, and check their answer simply by lifting the construction paper bush.

Not only did this experience offer children continued opportunities for problem solving, it helped them to see the connection among their own playground experiences, mathematics, and literacy. One 4-year-old child commented to the teacher after returning from outdoor play, "It is a good thing you have us around, 'cause you have so many problems! You really need our help!" These children are becoming powerful problem solvers!

Reasoning

Reasoning is the heart of mathematics. It means thinking through a question or a problem to arrive at an answer. Young children can and do reason. When presented with a problem or question, they make conjectures or guesses and then, in their own way, justify them. Their justifications often seem illogical, and they are not always aware of how they arrived at their answers. Preschool children are just beginning to make sense of mathematical situations. As they experience more and more mathematics, their understanding and reasoning skills develop.

Teaching and Encouraging Reasoning

Preschool children need experiences to help them develop and clarify their thinking. Here are important strategies for promoting children's reasoning skills:

Observe and listen to children in order to interact in ways that promote reasoning. Begin by observing children and listening to them talk as they work and interact with peers. As children make predictions, classify objects, or identify patterns, ask them to explain why they think as they do or why they made a choice between one idea and another. Listen thoughtfully to their responses. Their initial response may be, "Because," or they may simply shrug their shoulders. Regardless of the responses, persist in encouraging children's justifications and reasoning. With continued experience, children learn to verbalize their reasoning and justify their ideas more clearly and concisely.

Children know that you value their ideas by the way you respond, including the way you listen to them. Listening to each child's reasoning, encouraging children to listen to one another's justifications, asking relevant questions, and sharing your reasoning are ways to scaffold children's learning.

Plan reasoning experiences. Reasoning can be encouraged by offering activities that invite children to make conjectures, to explore and investigate their ideas, and to explain or justify their beliefs. Examples of such activities include classification activities that require children to look for similarities and differences among objects, or prediction activities that require children to identify and extend patterns.

Not is an important word that is essential to the process of reasoning. Classification systems require a child to understand what *is*, as well as what *is not*. For example, children who are wearing jackets with hoods can be identified as well as children who are *not* wearing jackets with hoods. Objects that are red can be identified as well as objects that are *not* red. It is important to use the word *not* in daily conversation and to introduce other words that are important to reasoning, such as *or, if, then, because, none, some, all, never,* and *probably.*

A Routine Example of Reasoning: "Inside the Circle"

Classification activities require the use of reasoning and are routinely enjoyed by children. Initially, young children classify sets of objects randomly, seemingly with no reasoning at all. They simply put things together in a group because they *like them* or the things *are special*. Children then begin to group objects by using one attribute for classification (e.g., they are all blue; they all have three corners; they all have wheels). They later realize that an object may be classified in more than one way (e.g., an object can have corners and be blue and have wheels). Finally, children can view objects that have already been classified and identify the rule that places them in a particular group.

A favorite classification game of preschool children is called "Inside the Circle." To play, the teacher classifies a group of objects by one "secret" attribute. She forms a circle on the floor with a piece of yarn and then places the objects that have the secret attribute *inside* the circle. The objects that do not have the secret attribute are placed *outside* or *not inside* the circle. The children's task is to identify the secret attribute by using the objects as clues. To do this, the children must use their reasoning skills, identify similarities and differences between objects *inside* the circle and *not inside* the circle, and verbalize the classification rule.

Consider what happens one day when a group of 4-year-old children play "Inside the Circle." It is midyear, and the children have played "Inside the Circle" many times, using color as the sorting rule. They also played once when the three-dimensional shape *sphere,* or *ball,* was the sorting rule.

Ms. Tory, the teacher, places a poster with a large circle drawn in the middle of it on the floor where all of the children can see it.

Ms. Tory: *Today we will play our game with shapes. Remember, your job is to be a detective and figure out what shapes go inside the circle. Then, if you are really a good detective, you can use words to tell me what those shapes are called. Remember, a good detective doesn't guess until he gets some clues. Here are the first clues.* (Ms. Tory places a red triangle inside the circle and a red circle outside the circle. Children begin talking to each other and quietly saying answers. After a minute, Ms. Tory places a thin blue triangle inside the circle and a blue octagon outside the circle. She is quiet as children begin talking.)

Ms. Tory: *Now talk to a partner and see whether you can tell me what my word or rule might be.*

There is a buzz in the room as most children discuss what the sorting rule could be. Some children sit silently.

Children: *It's red. It's blue. It's a rectangle. It's not a circle. It has points. It only has three points.*

Ms. Tory: *Now let me give you some more clues. Watch carefully.* (Ms. Tory places two green triangles inside the circle in a rather random position. They are not equilateral triangles; one is long and thin, and the other is short and thick. She then places another green shape that is not a triangle outside the circle.) *Talk with your partner again and see if you can figure out what my word might be.*

The children talk among themselves. Some try to get Ms. Tory's attention to tell her what they think. She listens but does not respond to their ideas. She simply points to other children, indicating that they should explain their reasoning to their friends.

Ms. Tory: *Now we are ready to test your answers. Remember, we listen to everyone's answer. There may be more than one way to tell about the shapes that are inside the circle! What do you think?*

Setsuko: *It's pointy.*

Ms. Tory: *You're really thinking. Can you show us the points on the shapes?* (Setsuko touches the shapes' points.) *What about the shapes outside the circle? Remember, they can't have any points! Do you see any points there?*

Setsuko: (Shrugs and looks puzzled. Ms. Tory pretends to be puzzled also.)

Dallas: *I think it is green.*

Ms. Tory: *Another idea! Can you point out the shapes that are green and inside the circle?* (Dallas points to the two green triangles inside the circle. He looks at the other green shape outside the circle and points to it as well.) *Hmmm. There are two green shapes inside the circle, but there is also a green shape outside the circle. Let's look at all the shapes inside the circle. How are they all alike? What do they have that is the same?* (Again, Ms. Tory allows time for children to talk to their peers.)

Crystal: *There are three points.*

Leo: *And three sides.*

Ms. Tory: *Oh, some other ideas! Let's check!* (Children check each shape inside the circle and identify the ones that have three points and three sides.) *Now we must check the shapes outside the circle. They must not have three points, and they must not have three sides.* (Children check each shape, and the teacher makes sure she uses the word *not.*)

Ms. Tory: *Any other ideas?* (The process is repeated for the other guesses. All answers are checked and demonstrated, with children explaining their answers each time.)

Ms. Tory: *Now we need many more shapes on our poster.* (She distributes many paper shapes to the children, and they use glue sticks to place the triangles inside the circle and the other shapes outside the circle.)

Sonya: *Can we do more?*

Ms. Tory: *Absolutely! Where should we put the poster so you can add more shapes?*

Leo:	*How about the Art area? There is paper and glue there already!*
Children:	*Yeah! The Art area is a good place.*
Ms. Tory:	*Okay, we'll put the poster in the Art area. Your job is to add more shapes to our poster. If a shape fits our rule, glue it inside the circle. If it does not fit our rule, glue it outside the circle. Remember to check your reasons before you glue a shape.*

The poster is then placed in the Art area, where children can draw or trace their own shapes, cut them out, and glue them on the poster. At the end of the day, the class reviews the shapes on the poster. The descriptive labels—*triangles, 3 points, 3 lines*—are written on the poster.

Note that not all of the children were able to identify the common attribute of the shapes inside the circle. However, after working with many shapes and classifying them by using the children's terms, they have a much better understanding of the geometric concept of *triangle*. With repeated experiences such as this one, children's reasoning skills develop.

Communication

Communication is the sharing of thoughts, ideas, and feelings with others. We communicate in many ways: through gestures, facial expressions, drawings, writing, and speaking. Children are often adept at communicating, but, when they begin communicating about mathematics, their ideas and thoughts are often unorganized and undeveloped. This is because they do not have the language of mathematics or an understanding of the symbols that represent particular concepts.

Teachers can help children learn to communicate mathematically by encouraging them to share their ideas orally, visually, and symbolically. Teachers also clarify or restate children's ideas with mathematical language and symbols. The more opportunities children have to share their ideas as well as listen to other children's ideas and strategies, the better they become at verbalizing their mathematical understandings and connecting their informal understanding with more formal, school-based mathematics.

Teaching and Encouraging Communication

Teaching for communication involves equipping the children with the tools and skills they need to communicate their mathematical ideas. Here are important strategies for promoting children's communication:

Provide tools for communication. Writing and drawing tools and a variety of paper and other writing surfaces should be a part of every interest area. In addition, resources that include numerals, symbols, measurements, and spatial drawings should be displayed and incorporated into the environment as well as integrated with topics of study. Include such items as newspaper or magazine ads, signs, blueprints, phone books, catalogs, size labels, and receipt pads. Both real and toy communication tools, such as audio recorders, phones, and microphones, should also be included because they promote speaking and listening. Finally, tools such as rulers, scales, weights, magnifying glasses, computers, the Internet, or cameras can be made available for children to explore. All of these items can encourage children's mathematical communication.

Interact in ways that promote communication among children and between the teacher and children. Tools alone will not teach children how to communicate mathematically. Teachers must interact with children as they use these tools, listening attentively, asking questions, restating concepts, and describing processes. Suggestions for ways in which teachers can prepare the environment and interact with children to encourage communication can be found in chapter 24, "Mathematics Learning in Interest Areas and Outdoors."

Provide time and opportunity for children to communicate. Children learn to communicate only if time and opportunities to do so are available. In a child's early years, family members and others encourage communication and express great delight when children say their first recognizable words. As children enter more organized or formal school settings, their opportunities to communicate freely are often restricted or limited. If children are to develop communication skills, teachers must honor communication by listening attentively to children, encouraging conversations and peer interactions, and creating an environment that conveys the message, "Your ideas are important."

Encourage the use of a variety of communication resources. Teachers must introduce and encourage the use of a variety of communication resources: visual (e.g., pictures, drawings, photos, sketches, diagrams, software programs, and stamps); oral (e.g., audio recordings, children's voices, dramatic productions, phone conversations); and kinesthetic (e.g., mime, play dough, objects, sculptures, and blocks).

Emphasize the communication of mathematical ideas. Teachers must specifically emphasize the communication of mathematical ideas. To encourage mathematical communication, numerical and spatial tools as well as standard (e.g., measuring tapes, rulers and meter sticks, balancing scales, number lines, charts, and graphs) and nonstandard tools (e.g., blocks, counters, links, and yarn) must be evident and accessible to children. When teachers model the use of these materials and children have opportunities to experiment with these tools, children learn to communicate mathematically.

A Routine Example of Communication: "Calling Houston Central"

An inexpensive cordless microphone became a unique communication instrument for one group of preschool children. Every day, a child would pretend to be an astronaut calling the classroom from the "space station," which was an area behind a file cabinet. Using the microphone, the child would say, "Calling Houston Central! Calling Houston Central!" The astronaut would then give oral instructions to other children about how to use a particular item or material. For example, one week the astronaut directed the children to use play dough to create the three-dimensional objects he described. Another week, the astronaut had children create pictures with attribute blocks. Still other children told stories involving the use of counters and particular mathematical operations.

Initially, the teacher played the role of the Mission Control agent, interpreting and clarifying some of the astronaut's communication. Later, children became quite good at communicating the details necessary for success. The children who participated in this activity over the course of the year, as an astronaut or as part of Houston Central, showed marked improvement in both their listening and speaking skills, and they learned important mathematical concepts.

Connections

Connections involve linking new learning and experience to previous learning and experience. According to NCTM, "The most important connection for early mathematics development is between the intuitive, informal mathematics that students have learned through their own experiences and the mathematics they are learning in school" (NCTM, 2000, p. 132). Several types of connections can be made:

- connections between math at home and math at school (e.g., counting in Spanish at home and counting in English at school, homework questions that involve the use of numbers at home, and using recipes from home in the Cooking area)

- connections between content areas (e.g., introducing mathematical concepts by using a story or a book, measuring the results of a science experiment, identifying patterns in a song, using circular shapes in a picture)

- connections between the components of mathematics (e.g., number and pattern—children create patterns by using numerals; geometry and measurement—three-dimensional shapes are placed in a box that is just the right size; geometry and data—identifying all the triangular shapes on a class scavenger hunt and making a graph to show the results)

Teaching and Encouraging Connections

To teach and encourage connections, teachers must first be aware of the many connections that are possible between mathematics at home and at school, between mathematics and other content areas, and among the components and process skills of mathematics.

Teachers also should know that young children rarely, if ever, see their learning as "mathematics." Instead, their experiences are categorized as "home stuff" or "school work" or "choice time" or "outdoor time." Teachers must intentionally and explicitly call attention to the connections. Phrases like these can be used frequently to help children make connections: "This is like…," "Do you remember when we…?," "I think we did something like this…," or "How do you do this at home?"

Although a teacher's language highlights connections for the child, the most important connection words are the child's. When a child says, "Look, there's a pattern on the wall!" or "I see a triangle on top of the trash can!" or "Our house has more windows than the school 'cause I counted!" we know that the child is making connections. Here are important strategies for helping children see connections between mathematics and their world:

Label ideas and activities by using mathematical vocabulary. Connections can be made quite naturally, particularly during choice time when children are free to choose where, with what, and with whom they want to play. During choice time, a teacher thoughtfully observes children and then determines whether, how, and when to interact with them. A skillful teacher uses this time as an opportunity to talk about situations by using mathematical vocabulary (e.g., "We will need to use numbers to tell how many cupcakes we need for the party," or "I see you've sorted and folded the laundry. Do you help your mom do that at home?"). They also highlight the use of mathematical tools, such as the timer or measuring cups in the Cooking area, the balance scale in the Discovery area, and the calendar in the Dramatic Play area.

Include and highlight mathematics in activities across a variety of contexts. During choice time, teachers also pay attention to materials and activities that are relevant to mathematics, and they explicitly identify and expand upon them. For example, after noticing that several children are deeply engaged in block building and will probably not want to dismantle their construction, the teacher suggests that they draw a sketch of their building similar to the blueprints architects and builders use. She also offers to take a digital photograph of their construction as another way to preserve their work. She reminds them that they can use the sketch and photograph to rebuild their structure at another time. Not only are these suggestions satisfying to the children, the teacher has helped them make a connection between their work, the real world, and representation, which is an important process skill.

Teachers also help children understand the connections between mathematics and other content areas, for example, science. As children pour liquids for an experiment, observe their bean plants, or feed the class pet, teachers can encourage them to measure and record their ideas and findings in journals, on chart, or on graphs. Similarly, the teacher who hears children singing *The Ants Go Marching* and encourages them to act out the counting song will help children make the connection between music and math (e.g., "There's a pattern in our song!") Reading the book *The Ants Go Marching* (Sandra D'Antonio) connects math and literacy.

A Routine Example of Connections: The "Snake Game"

Games that facilitate connections are important in the early childhood classroom. One of the children's favorite games is the "Snake Game." Children play this game as partners, and the communication process is emphasized as children help each other remember the rules and how to count correctly. Mathematically, the "Snake Game" facilitates connections between many different number and operation topics. As children play this game, they discover properties of zero, practice one-to-one correspondence, begin to estimate, and identify specific numerical patterns.

The "Snake Game" was originally played in South America by using easily obtained pea pods as snakes and peas as counters and tokens. In classrooms, the snake is outlined on a game board and divided into about 25 sections. It looks something like this:

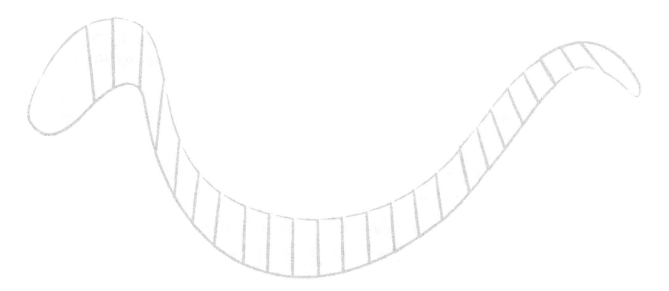

The "Snake Game" is played by two children at a time. Each child receives a token and three counters. To play the game, the children place their tokens on the snake's tail with the goal of reaching the snake's head. To begin the game, the first player puts zero, one, two, or three counters in his hand and hides the remaining counters. The second player tries to guess the number of counters that are in her partner's hand. If she guesses correctly, she moves that number of spaces. For example, if the first player is holding three counters and the second player guesses three, the second player gets to move three spaces. If the second player guesses incorrectly, the first player (the one holding the counters) gets to move that number of spaces (in this case, three). The game continues, with players taking turns until one reaches the head of the snake.

Initially, preschool children play this game with a teacher, an adult volunteer, or an older child. As they play, they learn the rules and become experts at following them consistently. Later, when they begin to play with peers, their reasoning becomes amazingly logical. After watching young children play the "Snake Game" many times, teachers noted the following generalizations:

- After just a few plays, children begin consistently to put three counters in their hands. They quickly realize that, if their partners guess wrong, they will get to move three spaces.

- Almost as quickly, children recognize that their partners are going to put three counters in their hands, and they begin consistently to guess three. Thus, the guessers are always correct, and they get to move three spaces. Play goes back and forth, with each player moving three spaces.

- After the children recognize the pattern of three moves, they begin to try to fool each other by putting different numbers of counters into their hands. Play continues for many moves, with children changing the number of counters at each turn as they try to fool each other.

- Eventually (normally after three or four games), one child decides not to put any counters in his hand. The other child never guesses zero, and the first child gets very excited because his partner has been fooled. However, the excitement quickly ends when he realizes that zero means no moves. When zero is used in other classroom experiences, children often connect it to their experience in the "Snake Game."

Children love to play the "Snake Game" at school and at home with family members. They especially enjoy fooling their partners. Each time they play, they are not only having fun, they are learning important mathematical skills and concepts: one-to-one correspondence; identifying sets of one, two, and three without counting; guessing the number of counters held; and, of course, making connections.

Representation

Young children represent, or show their thoughts about, mathematical ideas in different ways and with a variety of tools. Sometimes they draw or use tally marks or other symbols to explain or represent their ideas. Other times, they use blocks, counters, cutouts, or even their own fingers. Some representations require that children also give a verbal explanation so others can understand their meaning. Representations are essential to young children's understanding of mathematics. They help children solve problems and are useful to children when explaining their reasoning. Representations also make mathematical relationships more apparent to children. When combined with an explanation, representations offer teachers a window into a child's way of thinking mathematically.

Teaching and Encouraging Representation

Teachers set the stage for children to represent their mathematical ideas when they expose them to a variety of representations, including materials they can manipulate (e.g., advertisements illustrating various monetary amounts; maps; house plans; graphs; and toy cars, planes, or dinosaurs). Teachers also observe children as they work to represent their understandings, listen attentively to their explanations, and take photos when possible. Children need to know that you value their ideas and that it helps others to understand when they see a representation of some sort. Important strategies for promoting children's representation are discussed below:

Model the use of a variety of representations. The most important way a teacher can encourage representation is to model the use of various methods of representation. By doing so, they help children understand the way representations can be helpful in conveying different mathematical ideas, in explaining thinking and reasoning, and in solving problems. Modeling is an effective way of scaffolding children's learning.

Use questions, comments, and suggestions to encourage representation. Teachers also encourage a variety of representations with their questions, comments, and suggestions during interactions with children (e.g., "Show me what you mean… Can you make a drawing…use blocks…write numbers…? Tell me more about how…") Through these exchanges, children learn that representations can help them to remember what they have done and to communicate their reasoning. Teachers can provide opportunities for children to create representations for different audiences. Writing a counting or number book for another class, constructing a model of the playground by using blocks and craft sticks for the director of the preschool, or explaining the steps in making a favorite recipe to a parent volunteer are just a few examples of representations for different audiences.

A Routine Example of Making Representations: Children's Work

In a mathematically rich classroom, children's representations are displayed.

Photo of Sara's block pattern

"Down, up, down, up, umm, up, umm, up, umm, up." When Sara was asked why she said, "Umm," when the block was down rather than up, she explained that Patrick had taken all of the square blocks and she couldn't make the pattern the way it was supposed to be made.

Erin's drawing of block towers

When asked why her tower picture had a circular shape on top of a rectangular object, Erin said, "It didn't work like that! But it's okay. You can do whatever you want when it's on paper. It doesn't need to really work!"

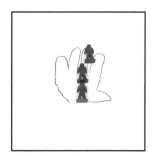

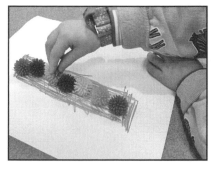
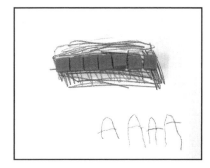

Each of these pictures shows a different measuring process and unit of measure. The first three show how children used various objects to measure the length of their outlined hands.

Three-year-old Jeremy's picture showing that he is taller than Mrs. Copley.

As you can see, a mathematically powerful environment is filled with children and teachers who make use of the mathematical process skills throughout the day, during routine experiences and planned activities, and in a variety of contexts. Problem solving, reasoning, communicating, connecting, and representing are all critical to the understanding of mathematical content. Children's unique ways of using the process skills make mathematics exciting for children and teachers alike.

Planning Your Mathematics Program

Planning Your Mathematics Program

Chapter 1 explains the components of mathematics. Chapter 2 explains the process skills children need and use as they develop and refine their mathematical thinking. In this chapter, you will see how the curricular objectives for development and learning help you think about the content and process skills of mathematics and understand how mathematics instruction takes place in *The Creative Curriculum* classroom. You will see how teachers purposefully and intentionally plan for children's mathematics learning and how they use the environment during daily routines and experiences.

In order to plan an effective mathematics program, teachers need to know the objectives for children's mathematics development and learning. As you read the at-a-glance chart that is presented in the next section, note the four objectives that are related specifically to mathematics.

Because children's mathematical skills affect and are affected by development in other areas, teachers also need to know the objectives for children's development and learning in those other areas. For example, verbal language skills are related to children's understanding of and ability to communicate mathematical concepts.

Objectives for Mathematics Development and Learning

The following chart shows the 38 objectives that are included in *The Creative Curriculum for Preschool, Volume 5: Objectives for Development & Learning*. They identify the skills and knowledge that children are expected to develop and learn before entering kindergarten. Objectives 20–23 are directly related to mathematics.

Objectives for Development & Learning: Birth Through Kindergarten

Social–Emotional

1. Regulates own emotions and behaviors
2. Establishes and sustains positive relationships
3. Participates cooperatively and constructively in group situations

Physical

4. Demonstrates traveling skills
5. Demonstrates balancing skills
6. Demonstrates gross-motor manipulative skills
7. Demonstrates fine-motor strength and coordination

Language

8. Listens to and understands increasingly complex language
9. Uses language to express thoughts and needs
10. Uses appropriate conversational and other communication skills

Cognitive

11. Demonstrates positive approaches to learning
12. Remembers and connects experiences
13. Uses classification skills
14. Uses symbols and images to represent something not present

Literacy

15. Demonstrates phonological awareness
16. Demonstrates knowledge of the alphabet
17. Demonstrates knowledge of print and its uses
18. Comprehends and responds to books and other texts
19. Demonstrates emergent writing skills

Mathematics

20. Uses number concepts and operations
21. Explores and describes spatial relationships and shapes
22. Compares and measures
23. Demonstrates knowledge of patterns

Science and Technology

24. Uses scientific inquiry skills
25. Demonstrates knowledge of the characteristics of living things
26. Demonstrates knowledge of the physical properties of objects and materials
27. Demonstrates knowledge of Earth's environment
28. Uses tools and other technology to perform tasks

Social Studies

29. Demonstrates knowledge about self
30. Shows basic understanding of people and how they live
31. Explores change related to familiar people or places
32. Demonstrates simple geographic knowledge

The Arts

33. Explores the visual arts
34. Explores musical concepts and expression
35. Explores dance and movement concepts
36. Explores drama through actions and language

English Language Acquisition

37. Demonstrates progress in listening to and understanding English
38. Demonstrates progress in speaking English

This volume of *The Creative Curriculum for Preschool* focuses on the mathematics objectives for preschool children. The appendix of this book includes excerpts from *Volume 5: Objectives for Development & Learning* that show the dimensions of each mathematics objective. They also show the typical progression of skill development for each dimension. Each progression shows a rating scale, indicators, and examples. Age-range expectations are presented in Volume 5, itself. Understanding each progression is critical to planning an effective mathematics program.

Keep the developmental progression for each objective in mind as you plan for each child and the group. Understand that individual children will be functioning at different developmental levels. You will tailor your strategies as you scaffold children's learning and help them move to the next level of the progression. The assessment information that you collect will guide you in determining each child's level and probable next steps.

Also recognize that children do not progress at the same rate. Some children learn new skills and behaviors quickly, while others need more time, practice, and experience before they move to the next level.

The Creative Curriculum for Preschool objectives for development and learning guide mathematics instruction and assessment, but teachers must also know how children acquire mathematical skills and build understandings about concepts. When teachers combine their knowledge of mathematics with their knowledge of child development and of each child's unique strengths and needs, they can tailor their instruction and support children's development and learning appropriately.

Guiding Children's Mathematics Learning

Like literacy learning, mathematics learning cannot be left to chance. Planning is essential. It gives purpose and direction to what takes place each day and helps to ensure that learning opportunities are maximized. A comprehensive, well-planned mathematics program addresses the components and processes of mathematics, and the classroom environment and materials. It also takes into account the children's abilities, interests, and learning styles.

As they plan for children's mathematics learning, teachers must decide what to teach, how to teach it, and when to teach it. They make these decisions on the basis of

- what children ages 3–5 should know and be able to do mathematically
- *The Creative Curriculum for Preschool* objectives for development and learning
- the strengths, needs, and interests of individual children

Good mathematics instruction requires that teachers use a wide range of teaching strategies. Children have unique learning styles, interests, and temperaments, and they progress at different rates. Some children love to make intricate designs with materials while others gravitate toward dramatic play or gross-motor activities. An approach that is successful with 4-year-old children may not work with young 3-year-olds. Additionally, the wide range of mathematical concepts and skills requires different teaching approaches. For example, movement activities are ideal for teaching spatial relationships; experiences with manipulatives are essential for teaching number concepts; and activities related to data analysis are done best in small-group settings. Because the environment provides the context for young children's learning, consider the ways in which teachers can create and use the environment to promote mathematics learning.

Creating a Mathematically Rich Physical Environment

Mathematical thinking is supported by a thoughtfully arranged, well-organized classroom environment. Focused explorations are more likely to occur in a well-organized environment.

A mathematically rich environment is full of interesting, novel materials. It fosters the exploration of important concepts in each mathematics component: number and operations, geometry and spatial sense, measurement, patterns (algebra), and data analysis. It stimulates children's thinking and entices them to solve problems, reason, communicate, make connections to what they already know, and represent their learning. In an environment such as this, children can discover patterns and relationships and pose new questions. Here are some basic principles to help you create a mathematically rich physical environment.

Strategies for Creating a Mathematically Rich Environment

Strategies	Examples
Organize space and materials.	Create orderly, well-defined interest areas.
	Have designated places for materials. Organize the materials and label containers and shelves.
	Place related materials in close proximity to one another on shelves (e.g., collectibles and sorting trays).

Strategies	Examples
Highlight the use of numbers, numerals, and other mathematical ideas (patterns, shapes, measurement) in displays.	Create meaningful displays, such as • birthday charts • attendance charts • class phone and address books • daily schedule • calendar of events • interest-area choice boards • instructions for completing jobs or routines (e.g., setting the table or brushing teeth) • class-made charts and graphs • counting songs and rhymes • artwork and photos
Maintain routines so that children can begin to see patterns.	Upon arrival, children put belongings away, check in or sign in, and eat breakfast.
Enhance all interest areas with mathematics materials.	Include tools, manipulatives, and pictorial and symbolic materials (e.g., blocks, counters, collectibles, dice, dominos, timers, graphs, balance scale, number chart, felt or magnetic numerals, tape measure, rulers). Incorporate math-related environmental print appropriate to each area (e.g., telephone book, price tags, and calendar in the Dramatic Play area and signs throughout the room). Include appropriate mathematics books in each interest area (e.g., *Icky Bug Counting Book* by Jerry Pallotta in the Discovery area; *Shoes, Shoes, Shoes* by Ann Morris in the Dramatic Play area). Provide writing, construction, and other materials in each interest area for children to represent their learning and record observations.

Materials and displays alone do not make the environment mathematically rich. Mathematics must be incorporated thoughtfully into events throughout the day. Children need to see ways in which mathematics is used in meaningful situations. For example, posting and referring to the daily schedule throughout the day teaches children about time and sequence.

Integrating Mathematics Throughout the Day

Most young children enter school having already been involved in a range of mathematical experiences, most of which occur naturally during their day. Mobile infants explore spatial relationships as they navigate the space around them. They crawl and climb over, under, and around objects, and then they position themselves so they can reach a toy. Toddlers learn about shape and size as they explore blocks, stack them, and knock them down. Two- and 3-year-old children help family members sort laundry, cook, and set the table. Such activities involve sorting, matching, counting, and measuring.

Preschool teachers build on these experiences. They can provide children with meaningful opportunities to count; measure; collect data; and explore space, shapes, and patterns. They can nurture reasoning, problem solving, communicating, and representing all day long. Of course, some of these occasions arise unexpectedly, for example, when a child announces that she found an ant hill with "a million ants." However, chance occurrences are not sufficient; teachers must purposefully incorporate mathematical experiences in each event of the day. Here are some ways to do so. The ideas are discussed in greater detail in other chapters.

Arrival

Preparing the Environment

Create an attendance chart (e.g., *Who's at School? Who's at Home?*).

Post written procedures for routines (e.g., washing hands, toileting). Use numerals to indicate what to do first, second, third, etc.

Post instructions for class jobs that show math used in meaningful ways (e.g., *Feed Cottontail 1 handful of hay, ½ cup pellets, 2 carrots, and 1 bowl of water.*).

Interactions

Have informal conversations that facilitate mathematics learning and thinking (e.g., "You're wearing a new shirt today with an interesting pattern. Can you read it?").

Remind children to place their name cards in the correct place on the attendance chart.

Talk with children about routine procedures and what they do first, second, third.

Interact to facilitate mathematics learning and thinking (e.g., draw attention to numerals and encourage children to think, reason, and problem solve).

> *Remember, each person gets one napkin and one spoon. Can you tell me how many of each you will need?*

> *How many carrots does Cottontail get? Let's read the instructions together.*

Large-Group Time

Preparing the Environment

Refer to the attendance chart.

Post a math-related "Question of the Day" or "Problem of the Week."

Post a picture/word daily schedule.

Post a weekly or monthly class calendar to document and call attention to meaningful events or special days.

Prepare materials, including visuals (e.g., manipulatives, books and related props, charts, posters, pictures, tapes/CDs, or flannel board cutouts) for any math concepts you want to introduce.

Use puppets or props with rhymes and songs.

Interactions

Demonstrate and explain how the attendance chart represents each child and the total number of children at school and at home. Explain how you will use the numerical data (e.g., to complete reports and to plan for snacks and meals).

Read and review the "Question of the Day." Invite children to predict and later interpret the answers.

Refer to the schedule throughout the day. Talk about what the children will do *after* the group meeting, *before* lunch, etc. Use words such as *morning* and *afternoon* as well as *first*, *next*, and *last*. Discuss the plans for *today*. Review some things that the group did *yesterday*. Use a clothespin to indicate the current time of the day and have a child move it appropriately during the day.

Call attention to upcoming events or special days recorded on the class calendar. Discuss things that happened *yesterday* or might happen *today* or *tomorrow*. Record them on the calendar.

Sing, recite rhymes and fingerplays, and use movement activities that help children understand math concepts (e.g., number, shapes, spatial relations, and patterns).

Introduce new math materials and vocabulary.

Read math-related books. Use comments and open-ended questions to introduce, expand upon, or extend the mathematical concepts presented.

Play math games.

Invite children to share their math discoveries and questions.

Have a small group of children act out math word problems. The remaining children can help solve the problem.

Choice Time

Preparing the Environment

Create choice boards for interest areas that indicate the number of children who may be in a given area at a time.

Organize materials in ways that encourage children to sort and classify.

Equip all interest areas with mathematics materials (see chapter 24), particularly Dramatic Play.

Add math-related books appropriate to each interest area.

Add writing, drawing, and construction materials so children can represent their discoveries and learning.

Post step-by-step instructions for using equipment (e.g., computers) or handling routine tasks (e.g., cleaning up an area).

Add timers so children can learn about and manage their time in a favorite interest area or with a toy or game.

Interactions

Talk about the number of children an area can accommodate. Discuss how to figure out whether there is room for others.

Discuss ways to figure out where items belong. Note similarities and differences among materials and the ways in which they are grouped.

Interact with children on a variety of levels. Listen, have informal conversations, pose questions and challenges, model or demonstrate a process, give feedback, and offer clues.

Model and "think aloud" about how you are using a new material, your approach to solving a problem, or ways to collect and report data.

Read math-related books with individuals or small groups of children. Interact with children in ways that intentionally draw their attention to the mathematical concepts presented in the books (e.g., pose questions and problems, and help children make connections to what they already know).

Invite an individual child or a small group of children to work with you or play a game related to a particular skill or concept.

Encourage children to document, or represent, their mathematics learning.

Give children a 5-minute warning before cleanup time.

Observe children and take notes about children's actions, abilities, and use of materials.

Small-Group Time

Preparing the Environment

Prepare print or visual materials (e.g., recipes, song charts, and rhymes).

Add props, flannel materials, and storyboards for storytelling or retelling.

Prepare materials and supplies such as manipulatives, tapes/CDs, games, or writing materials to conduct a focused activity.

Interactions

Sing, recite rhymes and fingerplays, and use movement activities that help children understand mathematical concepts (e.g., number, shapes, spatial relations, or patterns).

Read math-related books. Interact with the children in ways that intentionally draw their attention to the mathematical concepts presented in the books (e.g., pose questions and problems, and help children make connections to what they already know).

Have children dramatize counting rhymes and fingerplays (e.g., *Five Little Monkeys Jumping on the Bed* by Eileen Christelow).

Tell stories that focus on particular mathematical concepts (e.g., Bill Grossman's *My Little Sister Ate One Hare,* which focuses on number and patterns).

Have children create mathematics books (e.g., number, pattern, or shape).

Present mathematical story problems that give children experience with number (quantity, joining sets, and separating sets), measurement, or geometry.

Play mathematical games indoors and outdoors.

Offer sorting and graphing experiences.

Informally assess children to determine learning strengths and needs.

Snack and Mealtime

Preparing the Environment

Post step-by-step instructions for routines (e.g., washing hands). Use numerals to indicate what to do first, second, third, etc.

Include snack and/or lunch helpers on the job chart (e.g. to set the table and pass out supplies).

Post self-serve snack charts and picture/word recipes.

Include cups, spoons, and other containers in a variety of sizes for children to learn about measurement, quantity, and capacity.

Interactions

Point out numerals and talk with children about the handwashing procedure and what they do first, second, third.

Pose open-ended questions to facilitate mathematics thinking and learning (e.g., "Do you have enough chairs at your table? How many more do you need?"; "Shall we cut the carrots into long sticks or circles?")

Read the self-serve snack charts and recipes. Assist children with counting, measuring, and following the appropriate steps in the preparation process. Use open-ended questions and comments as you interact.

Interact to help children make connections between mathematics and everyday experiences.

> *You have three square crackers and one round cracker. How many crackers do you have altogether?*

> *I see you sorted your snack mix. All of the square cereal is in one pile, the pretzels are in another, and the raisins are in another.*

> *Can you pour milk into your cup until it is half full?*

Create graphs (e.g., "Which color of apple do you want for snack: red, green, or yellow?"). Then have the children analyze the data.

Survey the children after snack (e.g., "Did you enjoy the apple cider? Yes or no?"). Then have them analyze the data.

Call attention to shapes, sizes, categories, and patterns of foods (e.g., "An orange is like a ball, Dallas. Another name for its shape is *sphere*..."; "Look at the pattern on the rind of this watermelon. Let's read it..."; "This piece of felt is a large triangle. Can you name the shapes of other felt pieces in this box?")

Transitions

Preparing the Environment

Think in advance about appropriate mathematical songs, rhymes, chants, or games to use.

Prepare materials you need for the activity (e.g., numeral cards, geometric shapes).

Interactions

Number (e.g., "If you have more than two pockets, you may get your coat.")

Measurement (e.g., "Make yourself as short [tall] as you can when you walk to the sink.")

Pattern (e.g., "Watch and do what I do as we go outside. Jump, clap, clap; jump, clap, clap.")

Spatial sense (e.g., "Go *through* [*under, around*] this circle [hula hoop] as you walk.")

Sorting (e.g., "If you're wearing something green, go with Mr. Alvarez for story time.")

Sing songs and recite rhymes, chants, and fingerplays that have a mathematics focus (e.g., counting: "One, two, three, four, five. I caught a fish alive.") and verbal, physical, or auditory patterns (e.g., "If you're happy and you know it, clap your hands.").

Outdoor Time

Preparing the Environment

Provide measuring tools (e.g., cups for the Sand and Water area; string or rulers for plants).

Provide equipment such as tunnels, traffic cones, balls, boxes.

Provide writing materials for children to use to record mathematical information.

Interactions

Use math vocabulary as you talk about ways in which children move and play.

Call attention to patterns and shapes in nature and the outdoor environment (e.g., the cylindrical shape of a pipe, the pattern on a caterpillar, patterns on a wall).

Talk with children about how they might sort and classify collections of natural materials. Invite them to make a graph when you return to the classroom.

Offer movement activities that help children explore spatial relationships (e.g., *go over, under, through,* or *around* objects) and measurement (e.g., fast–slow, heavy–light).

Introduce counting and pattern games (jump rope rhymes, hand jive, hopscotch).

Encourage children to look at and draw objects from a variety of perspectives.

Integrate math into projects or other experiences (e.g., measure plants to see how they grow from day to day or week to week; encourage children to make shadow shapes).

Rest Time

Preparing the Environment

Establish a rest-time routine.

Play music that has a slow rhythm.

Display a clock.

Interactions

Remind children of the routines and patterns of rest time (e.g., prepare their mats, get blankets, and use the restroom).

Use open-ended questions during preparation for rest time (e.g., "Where's your cot? Near the aquarium? Between Leo's and Crystal's cot?").

Talk about what happened before rest time and what will happen after rest time.

Use the language of time (e.g., *one hour* or *half an hour*) to describe the rest period. Let children see you referring to the clock to know when rest time is over.

Offer quiet activities with a mathematical focus to children who do not nap (e.g., stringing attribute beads, working with pattern blocks).

Departure

Preparing the Environment

Review the daily schedule and the calendar of events.

Prepare mathematical materials for children to take home and share with their families.

Interactions

Talk about the events of the day, calling attention to the time they occurred (e.g., in the *morning, before* lunch, *after* lunch). Ask the children to decide on one event of the day that they want to record on the calendar. Review what they chose to record *yesterday.*

Review important events about which children want to tell family members.

Call attention to what the clock looks like when it is time to go home.

Planning Learning Experiences

Teaching in the preschool classroom requires a range of approaches. Effective ways of introducing a particular topic or extending learning vary widely. This section begins with a discussion of child-initiated learning experiences and then offers suggestions for teacher-guided instruction. Examples of how to work with children during large- and small-group times and during studies are included.

Child-Initiated Learning

Young children are curious and eager to investigate their environment. As they play and interact with objects and others, they express and represent what they know and they make new discoveries. To fully grasp mathematical concepts, children must have repeated opportunities to participate in a wide range of activities and to use a variety of materials. They also need opportunities to discuss their observations and discoveries.

In *The Creative Curriculum* classroom, choice time is the segment of the day set aside for child-initiated learning experiences. Teachers create mathematically rich interest areas where children can manipulate and explore with materials, discover interesting mathematical relationships, discuss their observations with peers and adults, and pose new questions. Children choose where, with what, and with whom they work.

During child-initiated learning, teachers observe first and then decide whether, how, and when to engage with children to facilitate learning. They determine the type and level of their involvement with children on the basis of their understanding of early childhood mathematical skills and concepts and their knowledge of each child's developmental level. Examples of ways in which teachers respond to and interact with children during choice time are presented in chapter 24.

Teacher-Guided Instruction

In *The Creative Curriculum* classroom, teachers do not rely exclusively on child-initiated experiences to promote mathematical understanding. Opportunities to explore some mathematical topics may not occur during choice time. There are also concepts and terminology that children cannot discover on their own. A child may gain an understanding of the concept of one-to-one correspondence through repeated experiences with materials in interest areas. However, without being told, the same child may not learn what a circle is or that the numeral *4* represents her age. For this reason, *The Creative Curriculum for Preschool* offers a balanced approach to teaching mathematics, one that includes adult-supported, child-initiated experiences and instruction planned by the teacher.

Teacher-initiated instruction occurs most often during large- and small-group times and is used to teach new mathematical concepts or skills explicitly. Previously presented concepts are also revisited during group times to help children see connections among mathematical ideas. Teachers also help children apply what they know in a variety of situations and across content areas. For example, children can combine their knowledge of patterns and shapes as they make patterns with shapes (e.g., square, circle; square, circle; and so forth). Math and literacy are combined as children count and clap the number of syllables in each child's name.

Mathematics activities or lessons are planned by the teacher, usually with a particular concept or skill in mind. When they explore mathematics in meaningful ways, children learn more than the targeted concept or skill. For example, a lesson on measurement will also include counting, vocabulary, and fine motor skills. Flexibility is crucial in planning and in teaching. Teachers must continually monitor children's level of interest and understanding, be prepared to respond on a variety of levels, and be willing to incorporate the children's ideas into the experience. Well-constructed plans provide structure and direction, but they also allow for on-the-spot revisions.

When planning mathematics experiences, teachers must consider the developmental and individual needs of the children. Children are active learners. They should be physically and mentally involved, talking and reasoning, manipulating materials, singing, chanting, or moving about. All children, especially English-language learners and children with language delays, need manipulatives and visual materials such as drawings, models, and photographs. Consider various steps in your planning.

Before teaching, think about these questions:

> *What do I want children to know and be able to do?*
>
> *What do children already know about this topic?*
>
> *What essential dispositions am I fostering?*
>
> *How will I evaluate and assess the children's learning?*

During teaching, think about these questions:

> *Is every child learning what I expected?*
>
> *Is unanticipated learning occurring?*
>
> *Are things going as planned?*

After teaching, ask:

> *What worked? What is the evidence?*
>
> *What needs to be changed?*
>
> *What do I do next for the group as a whole?...for individual children?*

The following sections show how two preschool teachers, Ms. Tory and Mr. Alvarez, use large-group and small-group times to teach children about sorting.

Large Groups

The teachers bring children together as a whole group at multiple times of the day and for various reasons. The first group meeting usually occurs in the morning for the purposes of creating a sense of community, sharing news, and discussing plans for the day. Mathematics is not usually the teacher's primary goal for this meeting, but it can be integrated easily and naturally, as described in the earlier section, "Integrating Mathematics Throughout the Day."

Large-group meetings are also ideal times briefly to introduce a new concept or materials. In the example that follows, Ms. Tory uses large-group time to introduce the concept of sorting by two categories. The children have had numerous experiences talking about groups that have a particular attribute, such as a particular color, and materials that do *not* have the attribute (e.g., red and *not* red). The notes on the right indicate Ms. Tory's intentions and reflections about this new activity.

Ms. Tory brings a bag with red and blue objects in it to the meeting area.

Ms. Tory:	*I would like to talk about something that we'll be doing today and for the next several days. Does anyone know what* sorting *means?* (Children are silent.) *Do you ever help your Mom or another family member put things into groups at home?*
Crystal:	*I do! I help Mommy put my socks and things in one pile and Daddy's clothes in another pile.*
Dallas:	*My Dad had a big bucket of screws and nails. I found all the screws and put them into one can, and he put all the nails in another can. I had to be real careful because nails can hurt you.*
Ms. Tory:	*Hmmm. Crystal and her Mommy sort the clean clothes, and Dallas and his Dad sort the nails and screws.* *What else do you sort? Do you sort anything at school? What about at cleanup time?* — Acknowledges Crystal's and Dallas's responses and invites additional examples
Tasheen:	*We put all the blocks on the right shelves.*
Zack:	*And we put cars and trucks in one basket and the animals in another.*
Alexa:	*We put the dishes in the cupboard.*
Ms. Tory:	*Yes, you do all of those things. You sort lots of things at home and at school. When we put clothes in the right piles, separate the screws from the nails, and put all the same kind of blocks or toys together, we're sorting them.* — Reinforces connection between what children already know and the new term *I brought a bag of things for us to sort.* (Ms. Tory opens the bag and spills its contents—various red and blue items—on the rug in front of her.) *What can you tell me about these things?* — Uses concrete objects and a simple example of two colors to introduce the concept / Encourages children to observe and talk about what they see
Zack:	*I see a fire truck and a car and some markers and some LEGO® pieces.*
Sonya:	*I see a dish and an apple.*
Crystal:	*Some of the things are red, and some are blue.*

Ms. Tory: *You mentioned a lot of different things, and, as Crystal said, they're all red or blue. Let's sort these things by color.*

(Ms. Tory makes a circle on the rug with a piece of red yarn and another circle with a piece of blue yarn. She places the red apple in the red circle and a blue car in the blue circle.)

What else belongs in the red circle?

Encourages children to think and participate

Children: *The fire truck. The dish. The red marker.*

Ms. Tory: *What's the same about all the things in this circle?*

Acknowledges children's responses

Encourages them to generalize

Children: *They're all red!*

Ms. Tory: *So we could say they're all the same…*

Children: *Color.*

Ms. Tory: *Yes. They're all the same color: red. What belongs in the blue circle?*

Children: *The blue crayon. The blue LEGO® The cup.*

Reinforces the terms *same* and *different*

Ms. Tory: *Yes. All the blue things belong in the blue circle. They're all the same color: blue. They're different from the red things.*

We just sorted all these things. We sorted them by color when we put the red things together and the blue things together. (She puts the items and the yarn pieces back in the bag.)

Uses the term *sort* again and explains what they did.

Some of you may want to sort these during choice time. Ben, will you please put these in the Toys and Games area?

Provides opportunities for children individually and in small groups to practice the activity introduced during the group meeting

Let's look at our schedule to see what we are going to do next. (She points to the daily schedule posted on wall).

Demonstrates the use of the schedule to promote an understanding of sequencing and time

Children: *It's choice time!*

Ms. Tory: *Listen carefully. If you are wearing red, you may choose an interest area. If you are a wearing blue, choose an interest area.*

Reinforces sorting during transitions

In this large-group meeting, the class participated in a brief, teacher-planned sorting activity. Opportunities were then provided for the children to sort the materials independently or with friends during choice time. Through careful observation of children who are using these and other materials, Ms. Tory will be able to determine who can sort by color or another attribute and which children need further assistance.

Music and movement experiences are useful in promoting many mathematical skills and concepts related to numbers, shapes, patterns, and spatial relationships. In the scenario that follows, Mr. Alvarez brings the children together after choice time to discuss what they did in interest areas and to enjoy a music and movement activity. He also uses this time to reinforce the sorting concept that was introduced by Ms. Tory, his co-teacher, during the morning meeting.

Mr. Alvarez:	*Everybody was certainly busy this morning. Thank you for telling us about the things you did at choice time.*	
	Today we're going to use streamers as we move to music. I have one for each of you. Sonya, will you please pass out the streamers? (Sonya gives each child a red or blue streamer.)	Chooses materials that will remind children of the morning's sorting activities
	What can you tell me about your streamers?	
Children:	*They have a stick on the end. They are long. Some are red, and some are blue.*	
Mr. Alvarez:	*The stick on the end is called a* dowel. *Yes, the streamers are long.*	Introduces new vocabulary and validates children's responses
	Who remembers what we did with the red and blue things that were in the bag Ms. Tory shared at morning meeting?	
Dallas:	*We put them into two groups.*	
Sonya:	*Yeah. All the red things went in the red circle, and all the blue things in the blue circle.*	
Mr. Alvarez:	*Who remembers the word Ms. Tory used to tell what we did?*	Reinforces the word *sort*

Setsuko:	*Sort! I bet we're going to sort these streamers.*
Mr. Alvarez:	*That's right, Setsuko! If we want to sort the streamers and the people holding them, how should we do it?*
Leo:	*Have the people with red streamers stand over here* (points to where he is standing with his red streamer) *and the people with blue streamers stand over there* (points to the other side of the rug).
Mr. Alvarez:	*What do the rest of you think about that idea?*
Children:	*Yeah! That's a good idea!*
Mr. Alvarez:	*Okay, everyone who has a red streamer stand by Leo, and those with a blue streamer stand on the other side of the rug.*
	If you have a red streamer, let me see you wave it fast. If you have a blue streamer, wave it slowly.
	Now, everyone with a red streamer, wave it high. Everyone with a blue streamer, wave it down low.
	When I play the music, I want those of you in the red group to wave your red streamers high. Those of you in the blue group, wave your blue streamers low. You may move any way you want to with the music, but remember that red streamers should stay high and blue streamers low.
	Okay. Here we go! (Plays music for a few minutes.)
	Let's change! Keep the blue streamers high and the red streamers low.

Revisits a concept previously presented

Uses open-ended question to solicit children's ideas

Integrates measurement concepts

Integrates spatial concepts

Small Groups

While the types of experiences offered at large-group time can also be done with small groups of children, small-group time is usually reserved for activities that encourage children to explore concepts more thoroughly. In small groups, teachers are better able to engage each child, to differentiate instruction, and to make accommodations for individual needs and interests. Small groups also are an ideal time to observe children in order to assess their understanding of a concept or skill. When planning small-group mathematics instruction, remember that it should be

- brief (about 10–15 minutes)
- focus on a particular math concept or skill
- offered in groups that are flexible in size and makeup
- active
- hands-on, that is, materials of some kind should be used
- include informal assessment

Knowing each child as an individual is important for effective planning. To know children, you must carefully observe them as they work with materials, listen to them as they explain their thinking or talk about what they are doing, interact with them, and study their representations. Small-group settings enable teachers to know children better and then to scaffold their learning. The sections that follow show how teachers plan for and use small-group times.

In the two previous scenarios, Ms. Tory introduced sorting to the whole class of children, and Mr. Alvarez reinforced the concept by using music and movement. The teachers do not yet know about individual children's abilities to sort, so together they plan a small-group activity that will help them determine what children know and are able to do. Mr. Alvarez leads the first small-group activity. His reflections are in the right-hand column.

The teachers have prepared four bags, each containing five green and five yellow teddy bear counters and five green and five yellow 1-inch cubes from the Toys and Games area.

Has the necessary props ready

Offers objects as visual prompts

Mr. Alvarez:	*Do you remember how we sorted things into two groups the other day at morning meeting?*
Dallas:	*All the blue things and the red things.*
Mr. Alvarez:	*Yes, we sorted things into a group of blue things and another group of red things.*

Paraphrases child's response

Uses the word *sort*

I have another set of materials for each of you. (He gives each child a bag.) *Take the materials out and think about how you could sort them.* (He watches to see what children do.)

Chooses familiar toys (If the materials were novel, children would be given time to play with them first.)

(Ben puts one teddy bear counter on top of each cube.)

Ben sorts by identity and uses one-to-one correspondence.

(Crystal puts all the yellow bears and cubes in one pile and all the green bears and cubes in another pile.)

Crystal sorts by color.

(Dallas makes four groups: yellow bears, green bears, yellow cubes, and green cubes)

(Alexa watches Dallas and then also makes four groups.)

Dallas and Alexa sort by more than one attribute, putting items that are exactly alike together.

Acknowledges children's work

Mr. Alvarez:	*You sorted in different ways. Tell me what you did, Crystal.*

Asks children to explain what they did

Crystal:	*Well, some of the yellow things were bears and some were blocks, but I put all the things that were the same color together, as Ms. Tory did.*
Mr. Alvarez:	*You sorted the things by color, making two groups: a group of yellow things and a group of green things. Tell me what you did, Dallas.*

Acknowledges each child's explanation by paraphrasing what he or she said

Dallas:	*I put all the yellow bears here. Then I put all the green bears here. I put the green blocks over here and the yellow blocks over here.* (He points.)

Mr. Alvarez:	*You made four groups of things that are exactly alike. Tell me what you did, Alexa.*	Notes that Alexa copied Dallas
Alexa:	*I put the yellow bears here and the green bears here and the green blocks here and the yellow ones here.* (She points.)	Plans to observe Alexa on another day to see whether she can sort independently
Mr. Alvarez:	*You also made four groups of things that are exactly alike: green bears, green blocks, yellow bears, and yellow blocks.* *Tell me what you did, Ben.*	
Ben:	*My bears are on chairs.*	
Mr. Alvarez:	*You made a rhyme: bears and chairs.* (Laughs.) *You all did different things with your bears and cubes. Crystal sorted into two groups by color. Dallas and Alexa put things that are exactly the same together. Ben lined them up in pairs.* *Now, can everyone sort the bears and cubes into two groups: same color and different color?*	Uses the opportunity to talk about rhyming, although the focus was not literacy Reinforces the use of the term *cubes* Wants children to sort by the criterion of *color*, not just *identity*, which is an easier skill
Crystal:	*I already did that.*	
Mr. Alvarez:	*Yes, you did. See whether Ben would like some help with sorting them by color.* (Dallas, Alexa, and Ben [with Crystal's help] put their yellow bears and cubes in one pile and their green bears and cubes in another pile.)	Gives Crystal a leadership role (assisting Ben)
Mr. Alvarez:	*Can you tell me why you put all of these together?* (He points to yellow bears and yellow cubes.)	Provides children with another opportunity to explain their thinking

Alexa and Dallas:	*They're the same color.*	
Crystal:	*We sorted by color.*	Provides an opportunity to practice sorting according to an attribute other than color

Mr. Alvarez: *Now, please put all of the yellow objects—both the bears and the cubes—back in the bag.* Then figure out a way to sort the objects that are left.

(Crystal and Dallas put all of the green bears in one pile and all of their green cubes in another pile. Alexa watches and then follows their example. Ben makes a new design with his bears and cubes.)

Mr. Alvarez:	*Crystal, tell us what you did.*	Gives Crystal an opportunity to think through and communicate what she has done
Crystal:	*I put the bears together and the blocks together.*	
Mr. Alvarez:	*Are the things in this pile the same?*	Acknowledges Crystal's thinking and clarifies the process for other children
Crystal:	*Well, they're all bears.*	
Mr. Alvarez:	*They're the same because they're all bears. And the things in this pile?*	Reinforces the concept of *same*
Crystal:	*They're all blocks.*	
Mr. Alvarez:	*Yes, they're the same because they're all blocks.*	Emphasizes thought processes more than correct answers

All of you were really thinking today. Please put your green bears and cubes back in the bags.

It's time to go outside. Listen carefully so you will know what to do. If you have something green on today, get your coat and wait for me by the door. (Pauses until children get coats.) *If you have something yellow on, get your coat and stand by Ms. Tory on the rug.*

This small-group activity gave children an opportunity to participate in another sorting activity. In addition, Mr. Alvarez learned more about the children's skills. Now Mr. Alvarez knows that

- Crystal can sort by color and then re-sort by identity

- Alexa and Dallas are beginning to sort by color, although Alexa followed Dallas' lead

- Ben needs to be observed more to find out whether he needs support in sorting by attributes other than identity, does not understand the term *sort,* or simply prefers using the manipulatives for other purposes

Assessing children's mathematical skills by using *The Creative Curriculum for Preschool* objectives for development and learning enables teachers to plan successfully. In the next activity, Ms. Tory uses the book *Five Creatures,* by Emily Jenkins, with a small group of children. During weekly planning for small groups, she and Mr. Alvarez determined that the book would be a good way to expand the children's understanding of sorting.

This is the second time the children have heard the story. The first reading was for enjoyment and occurred during large-group time. Much of the discussion revolved around families, cats, and other pets. This time Ms. Tory will use the book intentionally to focus children's attention on the various ways the creatures are sorted. The story also provides a context for counting and exploring quantity. To make the experience active and concrete for the children, Ms. Tory uses people and animal figures from the Toys and Games area to represent the characters in the story. Join Ms. Tory and six children for a focused small-group time.

Ms. Tory:	*I have a book that I would like to share with you today. It's a book that I've read to you before.* (She holds the book so the children can see its cover.) *Who remembers the name, or the title, of this book?*	Reminds children of a previous reading
Children:	*Five Creatures.* (Ms. Tory runs her fingers under the title as the children read.)	
Ms. Tory:	*Do you remember who the five creatures are?*	Checks to determine whether children recall the previous reading and discussion
Children:	*The mother, father, little girl, and the cats.*	
Alexa:	*Two cats.*	
Setsuko:	*The people and the cats are all called* creatures.	
Ms. Tory:	*That's right. Now I'm going to read the book again, and we're going to look at all the different ways the creatures can be sorted and counted. It's like the sorting you did with the yellow and green bears and cubes. Do you remember how you put all the yellow bears and cubes together and all the green bears and cubes together? Then you mixed them up and sorted them again by putting all the bears in one group and all the cubes in another group.* (Children nod, "Yes.")	Gives children a focus for participating in the story reading Makes a connection to a previous activity
	I have some pretend creatures here. (She opens a bag and takes out figures of a man, a woman, and a girl from the dollhouse set and two small cat counters.)	

Juwan:	*Those are like the creatures in the book.*
Derek:	*But not really.*
Ms. Tory:	*How are they different, Derek?*
Derek:	*The girl in the book has orange hair, and the cats don't look the same.*
Ms. Tory:	*You really studied the pictures didn't you, Derek?* (Derek smiles.)
	The figures I have don't look exactly like the ones in the story, but they will do just fine.
	(Ms. Tory reads.) *"Five creatures live in our house. Three humans and two cats."*
	Setsuko, can you take these figures and show us three humans and two cats?
	(Setsuko takes the figures and lines them up: man, woman, girl, cat, cat.)
Ms. Tory:	*Tell us what you did.*
Setsuko:	*The mommy, daddy, and sister are the people. These are the cats.*
Ms. Tory:	*You sorted the creatures by putting the three humans, or people, together and the two cats together. How many creatures are there all together?*
Setsuko:	*One, two, three, four, five.*
Ms. Tory:	*So how many creatures do you have?*
Setsuko:	*Five.*
Ms. Tory:	*I wonder how the creatures will be sorted next.* (Ms. Tory continues to read.) *"Three short and two tall."*
Juwan:	*I know! Some are big, and some are little.*

Responds to Derek and invites him to explain his thinking

Ms. Tory could have asked the children to point to the pictures in the book, but she decided to use figures to make the sorting and counting activity more concrete

Asks a child to explain her actions

Supports the child by paraphrasing her response

Wants to be sure that the child knows that the last counting word tells how *many*

Ms. Tory:	*Yes, Juwan, we say that the big ones are tall and that the little ones are short. (Demonstrates differences in height by using her hands.) Will you show us three short creatures and two tall creatures with these figures?*	Introduces measurement vocabulary related to height
	(Juwan takes the figures and puts the man and woman together and the girl and two cats together.)	
Ms. Tory:	*Who's tall?*	Checks to see whether the child knows the terms *short* and *tall*
Juwan:	*The mommy and daddy.*	
Ms. Tory:	*Who's short, or **not** tall?*	Revisits a concept discussed previously: *not*
Juwan:	*The girl and the cats.*	
Ms. Tory:	*(Continues to read.) "Four who like to eat fish."*	
	Alexa, will you show us? Which ones do you think like to eat fish?	Gives each child in this small group a chance to participate actively
Alexa:	*I like fish sticks.*	
Ms. Tory:	*So do I! Look at the picture. Who's eating fish?*	Acknowledges the child's response but returns the discussion to the topic
Alexa:	*The mommy and daddy and this cat and this cat.*	
Ms. Tory:	*Can you sort the figures to show us which ones like to eat fish and which ones do not like to eat fish?*	Suggests that the child use concrete figures because they are easier to count
Alexa:	*Alexa puts the man, woman, and cats together.*	
Ms. Tory:	*How many is that?*	
Alexa:	*One, two, three, four.*	
Ms. Tory:	*So **how many** creatures like to eat fish?*	Again, does not accept counting as an answer to the question "How many?" Checks to see whether the child knows that the last counting word tells how many
Alexa:	*Four.*	

Ms. Tory:	(Ms. Tory turns to the next page where two cats are shown sleeping on the bed with the girl.) *Leo, with the figures, can you show us how many are sleeping on the bed?*

Suggests that children use the figures to discover the answer

Leo:	(Leo takes the two cats and the girl figure.)
Ms. Tory:	*How many, Leo?*
Leo:	*Three.*
Ms. Tory:	*Now, who can figure this out? If there are three creatures sleeping in the girl's bed, how many creatures are sleeping somewhere else?* (When no one responds, Ms. Tory offers a prompt.) *Look at the figures on the rug next to Alexa.*
Carlos:	*The mommy and daddy are sleeping in their own bed.*
Ms. Tory:	*I think so, too.* (Ms. Tory turns the page.) *How many of the creatures can button buttons?*
Carlos:	*Three. The people.*
Ms. Tory:	*Who can't?*
Carlos:	*Cats can't do buttons.*
Ms. Tory:	(Ms. Tory continues to read and discuss the pictures with the children.) *"Five who love birds."* Show me five creatures, Derek. (She continues.) *"…two who lick each other."*
Children:	*Eeauu!*
Juwan:	*Cats lick to wash themselves.*
Ms. Tory:	*"And five who sit together in the evening by the fire."* (She turns the last page.)
Children:	*The end!*
Ms. Tory:	*The creatures in this story were grouped, or sorted, in many different ways. Can you name some?*
Leo:	*The ones that like to lick each other and the ones that don't.* (The children giggle.)

Setsuko: *By how tall they were and who could do buttons.*

Alexa: *Those who like fish and those that didn't like fish.*

Ms. Tory: *You remembered quite a few ways the creatures were sorted. I'll put the book and the figures in the Library area so you can tell the story, yourselves, or make up a new story about creatures that live in your house. I can't wait to hear about the new and different ways you sort the creatures.*

Responds to children's ideas and follows through

Derek: *Can we get a boy and a dog?*

Setsuko: *And a baby?*

Ms. Tory: *Derek, why don't you take all of the dollhouse people over to the Library area? Juwan, will you find a dog in the set of animals and take that over, too?*

When used intentionally, books and stories are useful tools for teaching mathematics and helping children make connections between mathematics and everyday life. Small-group settings are ideal for these experiences, because they encourage children to make comments, ask questions, and stay engaged with materials and peers.

Studies

In *The Creative Curriculum* classroom, teachers use studies to help children build content knowledge and develop process skills. A study is an in-depth investigation of a topic children are interested in learning more about. Children find answers to their questions through firsthand explorations, and they have opportunities to practice and apply mathematics skills in meaningful ways.

Beginning the Study

To illustrate how children use mathematics to learn, consider the study that evolved in Ms. Tory's and Mr. Alvarez's 4-year-old class.

There was an air of excitement in the classroom as children pressed their faces to the windows to see new construction taking place right on their school grounds! Ms. Tory listened to what the children said:

"I wonder what they are going to build."

"I bet it's going to be a gigantic room that everyone in the whole world can fit into!"

"I think it's going to be another classroom for more kids to come to our school."

"My dad is a carpenter, and he builds stuff like that all the time."

She noticed the children's curiosity and interest in the new construction and saw the possibility of a study on buildings and construction. While children worked in their interest areas, she noticed children representing their thinking. In the Block area, Carlos attempted to build a gigantic classroom. Sonya used art materials to draw what she thought the new building would look like. At the group meeting, the conversation continued. Ms. Tory wrote children's predictions about the new construction and discussed their representations. She then asked the children how they thought they could find out about the new building. Children offered various suggestions and said that they wanted to find out.

At planning time, Ms. Tory and Mr. Alvarez discussed their observations of the children and concluded that buildings and construction would be a good topic of study. Their next step was to create a web of big ideas to identify the content children could learn. They started by brainstorming words related to buildings and construction and recording each on a separate sticky note. Then they grouped the words into categories on a piece of chart paper, drew a circle around each group, and labeled it. The labels identified the big ideas.

In addition to helping Mr. Alvarez and Ms. Tory identify important science, technology, and social studies content, the webbing process enabled them to identify important vocabulary that could be taught and to think about the many ways literacy, mathematics, and the arts could be addressed. They also reflected on how early learning standards would be addressed through the study.

A good study begins with what children know and then leads them beyond their everyday experiences. Ms. Tory brought in a collection of photos of different types of buildings: schools, office buildings, skyscrapers, garages, warehouses, apartment buildings, homes, thatched-roof huts, and stadiums. Then she led a discussion about them. The children wondered whether the new construction project on their school grounds would look like any of the buildings pictured. Ms. Tory listened carefully as they talked about the buildings and began a list of the things they wanted to find out.

She continued to add to the list each day as the children wondered aloud. The list of questions became the heart of their study. The experiences that Ms. Tory and Mr. Alvarez offered were designed to help the children find answers to these questions. Ms. Tory wrote a note to families to let them know about the buildings and construction study and to suggest ways they might participate. She was delighted to find out that many family members were involved in construction work and were eager to come to the class to share their skills with the children.

What We Want to Find Out About Our New Building

What is it going to be?

How long will it take to build it?

Who is going to build it?

What will I be able to do in the building?

Where do people get the stuff to build it?

How big will it be?

Do you have to be strong to build a building?

What kinds of machines will they use?

Investigating the Topic

Ms. Tory and Mr. Alvarez first thought of possible experiences that could help the children find answers to their questions and gain deeper understandings about buildings and the construction process. The following were some of their ideas for incorporating mathematical skills.

Building and Construction Experiences	Ways to Use Mathematical Skills
Visit to construction site	Take photos at various stages of construction. Create a timeline of the project.
	Create observational drawings, calling children's attention to the shapes of the lumber, pilings, bricks, roof, shingles, windows, etc.
	Create a graph of the various kinds of workers at the site.
Create blueprints and build structures by following them	Examine blueprints and learn how symbols are used for representing something else.
	Create a blueprint of a dream house.
	Use blocks or boxes to make a model.
Exploration of construction materials and tools	Weigh and measure (using nonstandard units) various construction materials such as bricks, lumber, and screws.
	Estimate how many strikes it takes to hammer a sheetrock nail into a piece of wood. Count and record results.
	Place measuring tapes of various lengths, a carpenter's ruler, a t-square, metal rulers, squares, etc. in the Block or Discovery area or with woodworking materials.
	Use small ceramic tiles to create patterns.
Classroom visits from construction workers and other experts	Ask a parent to lead a simple woodworking project. Emphasize math skills, e.g., counting, comparing, measuring, and spatial relations.
	Use ordinal numbers to repeat a sequence of steps in a project, e.g., "First, you nail the sheetrock to the studs. Second, you tape over the seams. Third, you spread sheetrock mud on it. Fourth, you sand it. Fifth, you paint it."

Walk in community to examine various buildings	Count the features of various buildings, e.g., the number of doors, windows, floors, etc.
	Compare the sizes of buildings.
	Notice the patterns in the bricks, tiles, and shingles.
	Tally and then graph the different kinds of buildings seen on the walk.
Set up a building supply store in the Dramatic Play area	Sort and classify the materials.
	Create price lists for various materials.
	Use a scale for weighing nuts and bolts; use measuring tapes to measure wood.

There were far too many experiences to be completed in a week. Learning takes time. Mr. Alvarez and Ms. Tory used the "Weekly Planning Form" to record the materials they needed and to identify what they hoped to accomplish each week (see *The Creative Curriculum for Preschool, Volume 1: The Foundation*). They adjusted their plans on the basis of their observations of children as they engaged in the study.

Over the next few weeks, the teachers guided children through various investigations and activities to help them find the answers to their questions. They used comments and open-ended questions to help children clarify their plans, reason, solve problems, communicate, represent their learning, and make connections between mathematics and the real world. Here are examples of the questions and prompts they used:

"How can you make a square when you only have these triangular tiles?"

"I see you're building a wall but ran out of long blocks. How many shorter blocks would you need to fill the same amount of space as a long one?"

"This floor reminds me of the floor in our classroom. How are they alike?"

"Can you tell me about the house you built with blocks? I want to draw a blueprint of it without looking. Tell me what it looks like, and I'll draw it."

"How many tiles do you think it will take to make a floor in this room of your block house?"

Ms. Tory and Mr. Alvarez displayed documentation of the children's work during the study. The documentation included explanations of mathematical concepts the children were exploring and demonstrating.

Concluding the Study

To conclude the study, the children created a neighborhood of houses that were constructed by using blueprints they had drawn. They invited family members and other visitors to an open house similar to one hosted by a real estate firm. The children served refreshments they had made by using favorite recipes. They created ads describing their homes and the price of each. When the guests arrived, the children took them on a "home tour," explaining the features of their homes and how they were constructed.

As you can see, this study of buildings and construction enabled children to use mathematics in meaningful and relevant ways. It helped children to understand and apply skills related to number and operations, geometry and spatial sense, measurement, patterns (algebra), and data analysis, and to use mathematical process skills to gain a deeper understanding of the topic.

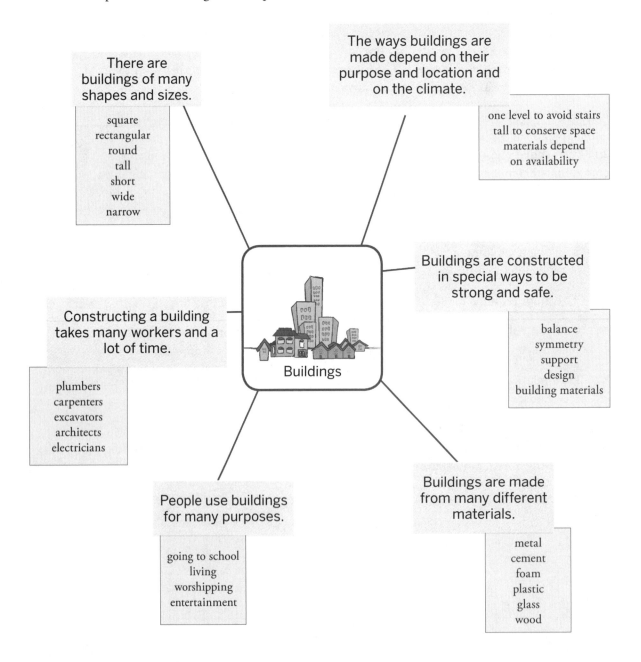

There are buildings of many shapes and sizes.

square
rectangular
round
tall
short
wide
narrow

The ways buildings are made depend on their purpose and location and on the climate.

one level to avoid stairs
tall to conserve space
materials depend
on availability

Buildings are constructed in special ways to be strong and safe.

balance
symmetry
support
design
building materials

Constructing a building takes many workers and a lot of time.

plumbers
carpenters
excavators
architects
electricians

Buildings

People use buildings for many purposes.

going to school
living
worshipping
entertainment

Buildings are made from many different materials.

metal
cement
foam
plastic
glass
wood

Meeting the Needs of All Children

All children should have opportunities to be actively engaged in mathematical experiences that are challenging yet achievable. Young children are similar to but also different from each other in many ways. They are all eager learners, but some are outgoing, boisterous risk-takers while others are shy, quiet observers. All children learn through active involvement with materials and other people, but not all children learn in the same way or at the same pace. In *The Creative Curriculum* classroom, the teacher's role is to determine what individual supports a child needs in order to participate fully. It is important to observe children carefully and continually, to see whether the current supports are effective and to make changes as necessary.

You will find that some children need additional support, perhaps including different activities or challenges. The sections that follow address ways to modify the environment and your interactions to meet the strengths and needs of three diverse groups of children: English-language learners, advanced learners, and children with disabilities.

Supporting English-Language Learners

Children who are English-language learners come to school with the promise of becoming fluent in two languages, but in the beginning they may find school an unfamiliar and bewildering place. The teacher's role is to provide an environment where all children feel comfortable and accepted while they develop and learn. Teachers do this when they provide cultural, social–emotional, and family partnership supports, as well as instructional supports.

Language plays a central role in teaching and learning mathematics. Words can help to anchor concepts, and questions can lead children to explore mathematical ideas.

Mathematical concepts can, of course, be learned in any language. Ideally, teachers support children's mathematical exploration in the children's home languages, but this is not possible unless you speak those languages. Fortunately, *The Creative Curriculum* classroom environment provides many nonverbal mathematical experiences. Children are not expected to learn mathematical concepts from the materials alone, however. Your interactions with English-language learners can also support their mathematics learning. The suggestions on the next two pages can be helpful in engaging children who are English-language learners in math activities:

Language Supports

- Keep your language simple. Use short sentences. Pronounce words carefully.

- Determine in advance a few mathematical terms that you want children to learn. Repeat these terms often.

- Use gestures and physical actions along with speech. You can show *big, small, fast,* and *slow* with hand and body gestures. Modify your speech to facilitate understanding (e.g., a loud voice for *big* and a soft voice for *small*).

- Show and talk. Use manipulatives, pictures, and objects (e.g., show a circle when talking about a circle; hold up four fingers when you say *four*).

- Sing, chant, and recite simple rhymes with the class. Repeat counting songs, finger plays, and chants.

- Let children respond in nonverbal ways (e.g., pointing, drawing, gesturing, acting).

- Encourage children who speak the same language to work together, communicating their thoughts and ideas in their home language.

- Open-ended questions may be difficult for English-language learners. Ask questions that can be answered with one word. Also ask questions that include the word needed for the answer (e.g., "Is this large or small?").

- Include English-language learners in conversations regardless of whether or not they respond verbally.

- Talk while doing. Describe what you are doing and what you see the child doing (e.g., "You're putting the red pegs in the red bowl and the blue ones in the blue bowl.").

- Listen closely. Make every effort to understand what the child who is learning English is telling you and check for understanding (e.g., "Do you want to put all of the cans on the top shelf and all of the boxes on the bottom shelf?").

- Story time may be challenging for children who are learning English. If possible, have someone who speaks the child's language read the book to the child before the activity. Learn a few important mathematical terms or phrases in the child's language. Read short books with lots of repetition and use gestures to support understanding.

Cultural Supports

- Provide books, charts, and materials that are related to the family's experiences and cultural and linguistic backgrounds.

- Learn and speak a few terms in the child's home language.

- Encourage the child to talk with other children who speak the same language.

- Post the daily schedule, signs, and labels in the children's home languages as well as in English.

- Sing or listen to audio recordings in the children's home languages.

- Teach or use the child's home language in whole-group activities. English-only speakers will benefit from these experiences as well.

Social–Emotional Supports

- Establish and follow regular routines so children can gain confidence, knowing what comes next and what to do.

- Smile and speak often to children who are learning English, but do not demand participation or a reply until they are ready to respond.

- Recognize that the amount of time it takes to feel at home in a new situation varies from child to child. Allow English-language learners to watch from a distance that is comfortable for them.

- Become familiar with the stages of learning a second language. (See *The Creative Curriculum for Preschool, Volume 1: The Foundation* and *Volume 3: Literacy*.)

- Provide many nonverbal ways for children to participate, such as through art, music, dance, dramatic play, and outside play.

Family Partnership Supports

- Foster partnerships with families, respecting their practices, inviting them to spend time in the classroom, asking for their advice about how to smooth their children's transitions, and keeping them informed about their children's activities (through interpreters if necessary).

- Help families understand how valuable it is for their children to speak two languages. Encourage them to support their children's home language by speaking and reading to them in their language.

- When possible, send home books and learning materials in the children's home languages, so that families can read to children and do learning activities in their own languages.

Supporting Advanced Mathematics Learners

Some preschool children are advanced in one or more areas of mathematics. These children do not simply use mathematical terminology or recite facts their older siblings have taught them. The advanced mathematics learner is one who may create complex patterns; build intricate, delicately balanced block structures; or love to analyze problems. It is important to celebrate and challenge children's advanced abilities, but keep in mind that these children are not always advanced in all areas of mathematics simultaneously.

All children need challenges tailored to their abilities and learning styles. Teachers plan for advanced learners just as they do for the children who need more time and assistance to master skills and concepts. Here are some suggestions for working with mathematically advanced learners:

Introduce data collection and analysis activities.

- Pose a question.
- Design a survey.
- Create charts or graphs.
- Interpret and then report results.

Introduce symbolic or more abstract math materials.

- Use dice and dominos.
- Introduce symbolic graphs and graphs with numerals along with graphs with concrete materials.

Introduce advanced computer programs.

- Look at the suggestions in *The Creative Curriculum for Preschool, Volume 2: Interest Areas.*

Integrate math with other content areas.

- Pose mathematical problems that enable children to use mathematical skills as they study other areas (e.g., "If the construction workers you see outside work 4 hours before lunch and 4 hours after lunch, how many hours do they work in 1 day?").

- Look for patterns in songs and talk about the refrains in books.

Focus on process skills.

- Pose more complex and meaningful problems (e.g., "How can you use the blocks to design a play yard for the guinea pig so that he gets exercise but can't run away?"; "How many more chairs do we need so that everyone can sit for the puppet show?"; "How can we divide the pizza so that everyone will have an equal amount?").

- Challenge children to think of new or multiple solutions to a problem (e.g., "Can you find another way to do it? How else could the man in the story solve his problem?").

- Encourage children to describe and explain their reasoning, probing and prompting if necessary (e.g., "How do you know these are all triangles? Did you count the sides? Did you look at the points?").

- Encourage children to represent their thinking and learning through drawing, writing, or construction. (e.g., "Here are four bears, and here are six cats. If I put them all together, I'll have ten animals.").

- Pose mathematical problems that enable children to make connections among the components of math (e.g., "Can you find a pattern in the numerals between 10 and 30? If our work packets go home every Friday, how many times will your families see your work this month? What about next month? Where might you look to figure that out?").

As you interact with children who have advanced mathematical abilities, you will discover their interests, find ways to share their enthusiasm, and identify strategies to address their strengths and needs. Continue to challenge children with advanced mathematical skills by introducing more complex materials and posing more difficult problems.

Supporting Children With Disabilities

Supporting the active participation of a child with a disability may mean adapting the environment or materials, adjusting routines, or modifying instructions. Some suggestions for general supports follow. For additional recommendations for an individual child, teachers should request assistance from special educators, the child's family, and—with parental permission—the child's therapist or pediatrician. Be sure to adjust supports as needed.

Environmental Supports

- Offer alternative seating options, such as sitting on an adult's lap or next to an adult.

- Use tape or carpet squares to help children identify the boundaries of their personal space.

- Provide appropriate assistive devices so all children can use the computer.

- Select software that includes auditory as well as visual feedback.

- Equip electronic devices, such as audio recorders and CD players, with switches that all children can use independently.

- Make sure that books and other literacy materials are placed where all children can reach them and put them away.

- Provide a range of manipulatives, puzzles, and other math materials that are interesting and accessible to all children.

Schedule and Routine Supports

- Preview activities with children who need help with transitions or new experiences.

- Break tasks and activities into smaller parts and provide verbal and other cues as necessary.

- Encourage children to participate to the degree that they are able.

- Use consistent, predictable routines to help children feel comfortable and secure. Introduce changes gradually to encourage adaptability and flexibility.

- Create a picture board with simple directions or reminders about how to attend during group activities or complete daily tasks (e.g., handwashing).

Tactile and Visual Supports

- Provide manipulatives that relate to the topic being discussed. For example, provide a set of shapes for a child to hold while the class is talking about the shapes on the flannel board; provide a large and a small block to hold while the class is discussing size.

- Attach a piece of textured material to the child's name card so that he or she can identify it by touch. Alternatively, let the child choose a special shape for his or her card, e.g., a circle, if other children's cards are rectangles.

- Introduce and reinforce math vocabulary while the child handles related manipulatives.

- Modify numeral cards or game pieces by adding raised dots to represent numbers. Raised dots can be made with glue.

- Include books with large print.

Language Supports

- Articulate clearly and monitor the rate of your speech.

- Repeat important directions.

- Use pictures. Create or purchase picture/symbol cards for basic mathematical concepts such as number (cards with a numeral and/or dots), shape, and size.

- Use pictures or objects to represent important concepts. Check for understanding often.

- Encourage children to talk about what they are doing as they manipulate objects.

Many of the suggestions for supporting English-language learners may also assist children with language delays.

Sensory and Physical Supports

- Select books and make or purchase charts with clear, simple pictures and familiar concepts.

- Observe to see what manipulatives a child finds easiest to handle. Some children may find it easier to manipulate magnetic numbers, shapes, and objects on a magnetic board.

- Determine what body position makes it easiest for a child to handle manipulatives and writing tools.

- Place large dots made with glue in the upper right-hand corner of book pages. This will separate the pages, making them easier to turn.

- Use Velcro® or magnetic strips on charts and graphs instead of using clothespins.

- When possible, have children use their bodies to experience mathematical concepts (e.g., have children hold hands around a tree trunk to form a circle).

- Offer a variety of writing tools, including markers, crayons, and pencils of various sizes. Place a piece of rubber tubing over the pencil or marker to make it easier to grasp.

24

Mathematics Learning in Interest Areas and Outdoors

Mathematics Learning in Interest Areas and Outdoors

The Creative Curriculum classroom is divided into interest areas where children spend significant time each day in child-initiated play. Full use is also made of outdoor learning opportunities. This design enables children to make choices, explore and experiment on their own, imagine and create, and interact with others. Interest areas are the ideal setting for children to actively and independently explore mathematical ideas and use mathematics to help them make sense of their world.

When each interest area is organized with mathematics in mind, children's play is meaningful and mathematics learning is maximized. By integrating mathematics into children's play, children have opportunities to reason; solve problems; communicate; represent their thinking and learning in a variety of ways; and make connections between components, with other content areas, and with the real world. Teachers carefully design and equip each area so that children's strengths, needs, interests, and learning styles are met and important mathematical content is addressed. Then teachers observe children and thoughtfully consider ways in which to interact to guide children's development and learning.

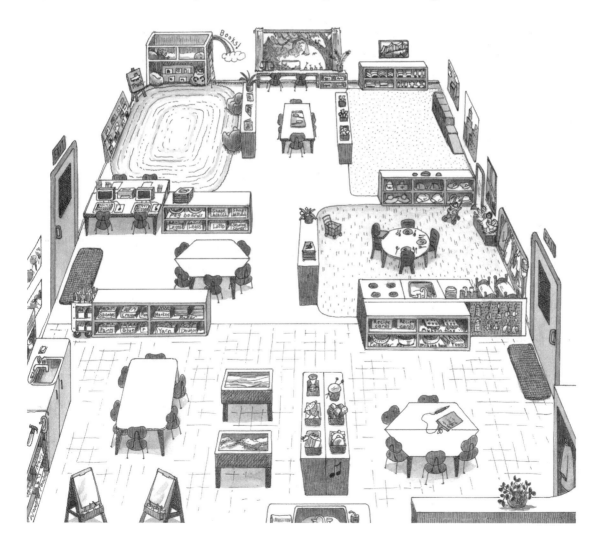

The Toys and Games Area as the Hub of Mathematics Learning

There are opportunities for children to explore mathematics in all interest areas, but the Toys and Games area is the hub for mathematical activities and learning. As children manipulate puzzle pieces, they learn about shape and spatial relationships. They use collections of objects, such as colored cubes, links, and other collectibles, to count and play number games, sort, make patterns, and measure. Teachers can support and encourage mathematics learning in this area by showing interest in and enthusiasm for children's work and by interacting in ways that prompt children to share their reasoning, solve problems, communicate their ideas, make connections, and represent their thinking and learning. Here are examples of how children's explorations in the Toys and Games area relate to the *The Creative Curriculum for Preschool* objectives for mathematics development and learning.

Examples of What a Child Might Do	Examples of Related Objectives for Development and Learning
Count a collection of buttons and say, "I have 10 buttons."	Objective 20. Uses number concepts and operations a. Counts
Roll two dice and say, "Four dots on this one and five, six, seven on this one. Seven dots altogether."	Objective 20. Uses number concepts and operations b. Quantifies
Put five counters on the numeral *5* card and say, "Five."	Objective 20. Uses number concepts and operations c. Connects numerals with their quantities
Toss a beanbag and announce that it lands outside the circle	Objective 21. Explores and describes spatial relationships and shapes a. Understands spatial relationships
Look at a puzzle piece and turn it several different ways to get it to fit	Objective 21. Explores and describes spatial relationships and shapes a. Understands spatial relationships
Make a chain; hold it next to a friend's chain; and say, "Your chain is longer. You have more links."	Objective 22. Compares and measures
Choose two colors of beads and make a bead necklace with a pattern of red, blue; red, blue; etc.	Objective 23. Demonstrates knowledge of patterns

Mathematics Materials for the Toys and Games Area

The Toys and Games area should have materials that encourage children to explore multiple concepts in each component of mathematics and use the mathematical process skills. As described in *The Creative Curriculum for Preschool, Volume 2: Interest Areas,* open-ended materials and collectibles such as buttons, shells, and keys are ideal for such explorations. Symbolic mathematical materials such as dice, dominoes, spinners, graphs, and numeral manipulatives are also important, because they prepare children for later abstract thinking. Books belong in this interest area, too. Many books present mathematical concepts in appealing ways and enable children to see mathematics used in real situations.

To highlight connections among materials, consider their placement. Place a book such as *The Button Box* next to a collection of buttons and a muffin tin to encourage children to sort. Display a shape poster and book about shapes close to the geoboards to encourage exploration of shapes. Remember, too many materials can overwhelm children. When selecting materials for the Toys and Games area, consider the abilities and interests of the children as well as important mathematical concepts. Rotate materials as appropriate. For guidance about how to introduce new materials to children, see *The Creative Curriculum for Preschool, Volume 1: The Foundation.*

Materials

- a variety of counters
- interlocking cubes
- connecting links
- 1" cubes or tiles
- matching games and materials (e.g., number, shape)
- collectibles (e.g., buttons, keys, natural materials)
- containers for sorting (e.g., trays, bowls, hoops, muffin tins, or clean egg cartons)
- pegs and pegboards
- stringing beads and pattern cards
- dominos
- attribute blocks
- pattern blocks, parquetry blocks, tangrams, pattern cards

- geometric solids (cube, sphere, cone, etc.)
- shape templates for tracing
- geoboards and rubber bands
- dice (e.g., with dots, numbers, shapes, or colors) and spinners
- numeral cards; cards representing quantities 1–10; number strips
- magnetic and/or felt numbers and shapes
- writing materials
- lotto and other games (e.g., number, shape, size, classification)
- balance scale
- graphing mat
- sequencing or seriation materials
- coins
- storyboards

Suggested Books

(Titles preceded by an asterisk are included in the Teaching Strategies Children's Book Collection.)

All About Where (Tana Hoban)

Barn Cat: A Counting Book (Carol P. Saul)

Beep, Beep, Vroom, Vroom! (Stuart J. Murphy)

*The Button Box (Margarette Reid)

*Button, Button, Who's Got the Button? (Trish Holland)

*Chicka Chicka Boom Boom (Bill Martin and John Archambault)

Cubes, Cones, Cylinders, and Spheres (Tana Hoban)

The Handmade Counting Book (Laura Rankin)

Let's Count (Tana Hoban)

The Line Up Book (Marisabina Russo)

More, Fewer, Less (Tana Hoban)

Mouse Count (Ellen Stoll Walsh)

One Duck Stuck (Phyllis Root)

One Monkey Too Many (Jackie French Koller)

One of Each (Mary Ann Huberman)

Only One (Marc Harshman)

Quack and Count (Keith Baker)

Spirals, Curves, Fanshapes & Lines (Tana Hoban)

Ten Dogs in the Window: A Countdown Book (Claire Masurel)

Ten Flashing Fireflies (Philemon Sturges)

Ten Little Mice (Joyce Dunbar)

The Very Hungry Caterpillar (Eric Carle)

Where Is That Cat? (Carol Green)

Where's That Cat? (Eve Merriam and Pam Pollack)

Using Toys and Games to Teach Mathematics

Children need time to explore the materials in the Toys and Games area freely. Through their playful manipulation of objects, they discover many mathematical relationships on their own. Teachers who carefully observe the ways in which children use materials and listen to them as they talk are able to determine the best way to respond and support their mathematics learning. At times teachers will ask a question, pose a problem, introduce a new term, or model the steps in solving a problem. At other times, they simply observe.

Talking helps children clarify and organize their thinking. However, young children are not proficient at expressing their thoughts, particularly if they are English-language learners. Your questions and comments can stimulate children's thinking, but be careful not to overwhelm them. Here are examples of what you might ask and say:

Number and Operations

"How many ducks are there? Are you sure? How do you know?"

"Can you make a chain with more links than mine? Can you make a chain with fewer links?"

"Which bear is first in line? Which bear is second?"

"How many shells do you need to put on this card?" (Point to the numeral *4*.)

"If you put two more buttons in the box, how many buttons will there be? How many would you have if you took one out?"

Geometry and Spatial Sense

"Tell me about these shapes. How would you describe them?"

"How many different shapes can you make by using these straws?"

"If you put these two triangles together, what shape would you make?"

"Can you find something in the classroom that looks like a can? How about a ball?"

"Can you toss the beanbag near the basket? Which beanbag is farthest from the basket?"

Measurement

"Which one is biggest (smallest, tallest, shortest, and so forth)? How do you know?"

"What else could you use to measure your tower?"

"Which shape can you cover with the most tiles?"

"How do you know which table block is the heaviest? Show me."

"Is this a picture of something happening during the day or at night? How can you tell?"

Patterns (Algebra)

"Tell me about this row of pegs. How do you know it's a pattern?"

"Can you finish this pattern? It starts out like this: circle, triangle; circle, triangle; circle… What shape should come next?"

"I'd like to make a pattern like yours. Tell me or show me how."

"Can you make a pattern like the pattern on your shirt?"

"How do you read this pattern? Can you read it another way?"

Data Analysis (Collecting Data, Sorting and Classifying, and Organizing Data)

"Which things do you think go together? Why? What name could you give this group?"

"How could we sort these buttons? Is there another way to sort the buttons?"

"Can you find all the cubes that are not green?"

"Tell me about those marks, or tallies. What do they mean?"

"What other pictures go in the animal column on our graph?"

Mathematical Process Skills (Reasoning, Problem Solving, Communicating, Connecting, and Representing)

"Why do you think…?"

"That's an interesting idea. What will you do next?"

"Are you sure? How do you know?"

"Can you explain that so that Keri can understand how you did it?"

"Can you draw a picture of that?"

Observing Children's Progress

As you observe children playing with toys and games, look for these indications of mathematics development and learning:

- using one-to-one correspondence
- counting
- using terms such as *some, all, more, less, more than, less than, fewer than, the same as*
- recognizing and/or writing numerals
- recognizing patterns of dots without counting (i.e., subitizing)
- answering the question "How many?" without recounting
- recognizing, describing, copying, extending, or creating a pattern
- using positional words (e.g., *over, under, in front of, next to, behind, outside, inside*)
- talking about how things are the same and/or different
- describing shapes (e.g., three sides, four sides, straight sides, curved, round, corners)
- naming shapes (e.g., *circle, triangle, square, rectangle, cube, cone, cylinder*)
- using comparative terms such as *big, bigger, biggest; faster, slower; longer, longest; same length; taller, shorter; heavier, lighter; holds more, holds less;* etc.
- using words related to time, such as *morning, afternoon, evening, night, day, noon, soon, tomorrow, yesterday, early, late, a long time ago,* etc.
- sorting
- using the term *not*
- keeping a tally during a game
- constructing a graph with assistance
- interpreting a graph
- explaining reasoning

Mathematics in the Block Area

The Block area is a favorite among children and one that presents children with numerous opportunities to explore mathematical concepts such as shape, size, space, pattern, and number. Children also acquire and refine mathematical process skills as they address problems such as how to steady a tower so that it does not topple, how to construct a bridge over a raging river, or how to make the roof stay up. Children can persist in solving problems when they are fully engaged in their block-building activity. Here are examples of how children's explorations in the Block area relate to the *The Creative Curriculum for Preschool* objectives for mathematics development and learning.

Examples of What a Child Might Do	Examples of Related Objectives for Development and Learning
Count and say, "I made a tower with eight blocks. See? One, two, three, four, five, six, seven, eight. It's eight blocks tall."	Objective 20. Uses number concepts and operations a. Counts
Add two blocks to a structure and say, "Now I have six blocks."	Objective 20. Uses number concepts and operations b. Quantifies
Identify a numeral in a counting book and count out that many blocks	Objective 20. Uses number concepts and operations c. Connects numerals with their quantities
Sit inside an enclosure made with hollow blocks and say, "I'm in my house."	Objective 21. Explores and describes spatial relationships and shapes a. Understands spatial relationships
Place two triangular blocks together to make a square and say, "My square has four sides."	Objective 21. Explores and describes spatial relationships and shapes b. Understands shapes
Try to make a door tall enough for a toy giraffe to get through and say, "The giraffe needs a taller door than the lion."	Objective 22. Compares and measures
Decorate the top of a block castle with a pattern: pyramid, cylinder; pyramid, cylinder; etc.	Objective 23. Demonstrates knowledge of patterns

Mathematics Materials for the Block Area

Many of the Block area materials suggested in *The Creative Curriculum for Preschool, Volume 2: Interest Areas* encourage mathematical thinking. That chapter also suggests ways to organize the area. The materials and books listed in the following chart also support children's mathematical explorations.

Materials

geometric solids

everyday materials
(e.g., cans, pipes, boxes, traffic cones)

maps

photographs of buildings and
other structures illustrating shapes
and patterns

photos of children's block
constructions, their neighborhoods,
and places the class has visited

floor tiles, carpet pieces

large pieces of cardboard

measuring tools

writing and drawing materials

Suggested Books

(Titles preceded by an asterisk are included in the Teaching Strategies Children's Book Collection.)

The Block Book (Susan Couture)

Build It From A to Z
(Trish Holland)

Building (Elisha Cooper)

Building a House (Byron Barton)

Buildings, Buildings, Buildings
(Judith Bauer Stamper)

The Busy Building Book (Sue Tarsky)

A Carpenter (Florian Douglas)

Changes, Changes, Changes
(Pat Hutchins)

Construction Zone (Tana Hoban)

The House in the Meadow
(Shutta Crum)

House, Sweet House
(Judith Bauer Stamper)

How a House Is Built (Gail Gibbons)

The Lot at the End of My Block
(Kevin Lewis)

Louise Builds a House
(Louise Pfanner)

*One Big Building: A Counting Book
About Construction* (Michael Dahl)

The Three Little Javelinas
(Susan Lowell)

The Three Little Pigs
(Bonnie Dobkin)

*The True Story of the Three Little
Pigs* (Jon Scieszka)

Unit Blocks

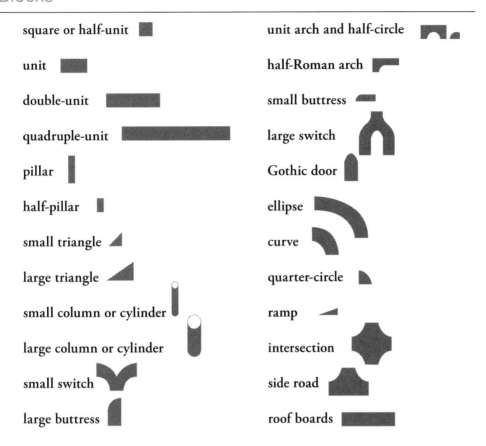

square or half-unit	unit arch and half-circle
unit	half-Roman arch
double-unit	small buttress
quadruple-unit	large switch
pillar	Gothic door
half-pillar	ellipse
small triangle	curve
large triangle	quarter-circle
small column or cylinder	ramp
large column or cylinder	intersection
small switch	side road
large buttress	roof boards

Using Blocks to Teach Mathematics

Understanding the developmental stages of block play helps teachers interact with children in appropriate ways (see *The Creative Curriculum for Preschool, Volume 2: Interest Areas*). For example, a teacher who observes a child pulling blocks off the shelf and piling them into trucks will recognize that the child is at Stage 1: Carrying Blocks. He is learning about the properties of blocks and gaining an understanding of what he can and cannot do with them. Knowing this and considering math content, the teacher may talk with the child about his choice of blocks and call his attention to their physical characteristics. She may try to interest the child in counting the blocks in his truck or matching them to the labels on the shelves when choice time is over.

Teachers first observe children in the Block area and listen as they talk about what they are doing. Then, using carefully chosen questions and comments, they introduce mathematical vocabulary, nurture children's understanding of mathematical concepts, and support their development and learning as serious builders, problem-solvers, and players in the Block area. Here are examples of what teachers might say as they interact with children in the Block area:

Number and Operations

"There are many people in your house. How many live there? How many are visiting?"

"This is the bedroom. Do these children share a room? How many beds will you need?"

"Your house has two floors: an upstairs and a downstairs!"

"That's a tall tower! How many blocks did you use to build it? How many would there be if you added two more blocks to the top?"

"What other objects are about the same height as your tower?"

"How many blocks do you think you used for the road? Did you use more for the road or the tower?"

"Can you carry five blocks to the shelf and put them away? Wow, that was easy for you! Can you carry six blocks?"

Geometry and Spatial Sense

"What other shapes can you make by using these four triangles?"

"How will you get from your house to Derek's gas station?"

"It doesn't look like there are any more of the longest rectangles. What other blocks could you use to finish your building?"

"That block is called a cylinder. It looks like a column in front of your house."

"I'm looking for blocks that have three sides. Next, I'm going to look for blocks that are curved."

Measurement

"Yes, your road is longer. It goes straight across the rug. Aisha used more blocks for her shorter, curved road."

"I think this tower is even taller than the one you built yesterday. What do you think?"

"I wonder whether it would take more tiles or more carpet pieces to cover the floor of your house. What do you think?"

"Will you car fit under the bridge? What about the truck? Will it fit?"

"You made a bed of hollow blocks that is long enough for you to sleep on. I wonder how many blocks you'd need to make a bed long enough for me."

Patterns (Algebra)

"I see you placed one block up, one block flat, one block up, and another block flat. If you keep repeating them, you'll have a pattern! What will go next?"

"I want to make a fence with a pattern just like yours. Will you tell me how to do it?"

"I'm making a pattern with unit blocks and small triangles. Can you help me finish it?"

"You created a patterned floor for your house with the tiles. Tell me about it."

Data Analysis

"You put all the double-unit blocks in one pile and all the unit blocks in another pile."

"Can you make a road that is the same length by using blocks of a different size?"

Mathematical Process Skills (Reasoning, Problem Solving, Communicating, Connecting, and Representing)

"Sometimes one road goes over another road, like on the freeway. How could you make an overpass for your highway?"

"What do you suppose would happen if…? Why do you think that?"

"How did you figure that out?"

"How is your shopping mall similar to the one in your neighborhood?"

"You worked very hard on your building. Would you like me to take a picture of it so we can remember what it looked like?"

Observing Children's Progress

While children are engaged in block play, look for these indications of mathematics development and learning:

- talking with peers and adults and describing what they built
- placing blocks or other objects in one-to-one correspondence
- using mathematical words such as *longer, shorter, inside, outside, square, triangle, round, more, less*
- describing size and position
- counting blocks
- making a pattern with blocks
- solving problems, for example, balancing a block or constructing a bridge
- matching shapes when returning blocks to the shelves
- comparing length or height
- describing or naming the shapes of some blocks (e.g., three sides, triangle, sphere, like a can, etc.)
- using two or more shorter blocks to equal a longer block
- constructing a structure that represents something (e.g., a house, car, or farm)
- arranging objects in a series (e.g., small to large)

Mathematics in the Dramatic Play Area

In the Dramatic Play area, children experience mathematics in ways similar to their mathematical experiences at home and in their communities. As they enact real-life situations such as setting the table, sorting laundry, or shopping for shoes, children use mathematics in meaningful ways and deepen their understanding of common experiences. They also have opportunities to solve real problems like determining how to divide apple slices equally among friends. Children's ability to engage in dramatic play, to imagine and recreate past situations, or to substitute one toy for another provides practice with abstract thinking and using the symbols of mathematics. Here are examples of how children's explorations in the Dramatic Play area relate to *The Creative Curriculum for Preschool* objectives for mathematics development and learning.

Examples of What a Child Might Do	Examples of Related Objectives for Development and Learning
Set the table with a plate and spoon at each place and say, "Everyone needs a spoon for the soup."	Objective 20. Uses number concepts and operations a. Counts
Put four candles on a pretend cake and say, "I'm four."	Objective 20. Uses number concepts and operations b. Quantifies
Count five coins when the cash register shows 5	Objective 20. Uses number concepts and operations c. Connects numerals with their quantities
Tell another child, "The store is too far away; we need a car."	Objective 21. Explores and describes spatial relationships and shapes a. Understands spatial relationships
Name the shapes of empty food containers and explain his or her word choice	Objective 21. Explores and describes spatial relationships and shapes b. Understands shapes
Look for clothes that fit a doll and say, "This dress is too big for my doll. I need to find something smaller."	Objective 22. Compares and measures
Tell a friend, "Every day is the same. First she gets her bottle, and then I put her to bed."	Objective 23. Demonstrates knowledge of patterns

Mathematics Materials for the Dramatic Play Area

In most preschool classrooms, the Dramatic Play area is initially set up like a home so children can enact the familiar roles of family life. As time passes, children's play extends beyond family life to include situations such as going to the doctor, a restaurant, or the post office. Mathematics can be integrated into any play topic by including materials that encourage children to count, sort, classify, and measure, as well as solve problems, reason, and communicate. Children who are experienced with dramatic play will enjoy using symbolic or abstract mathematical materials such as play money, a timer, a check book, price tags, recipes, or a telephone book.

An organized Dramatic Play area, with props arranged in labeled containers or displayed on hooks, promotes order and organization, which are important aspects of mathematics. The following chart lists mathematics-related props, accessories, and books for this interest area.

Materials

calendar	coupons
clock	measuring cups and spoons
timer	bowls, pots and pans, and wooden spoons of varying sizes
writing materials	
recipes	muffin tins and egg cartons
cookbook	clothes and accessories of varying sizes (e.g., socks, shoes, hats)
list of emergency telephone numbers	
phone book	wallets and purses
	newspapers (advertisements)

Suggested Books

(Titles preceded by an asterisk are included in the Teaching Strategies Children's Book Collection.)

Alfie's 1, 2, 3 (Shirley Hughes)

Anno's Counting House (Mitsumasa Anno)

The Big Brown Box (Marisabina Russo)

The Cake That Mack Ate (Rose Robart)

Caps for Sale (Esphyr Slobodkina)

Car Wash (Sandra Steen and Susan Steen)

A Chair for My Mother (Vera Williams)

Come Back, Hannah! (Marisabina Russo)

The Doorbell Rang (Pat Hutchins)

Suggested Books, continued

The Girl Who Wore Too Much (Margaret MacDonald)

The Glorious Day (Amy Schwartz)

Jesse Bear, What Will You Wear? (Nancy White Carlstrom)

Kevin and His Dad (Irene Smalls)

Mama & Papa Have a Store (Amelia Lau Carling)

The Mitten (Jan Brett)

Neighborhood Song (Trish Holland)

The Paper Bag Princess (Robert Munsch)

Peter's Chair (Ezra Jack Keats)

One Monday Morning (Uri Shulevitz)

The Quinceañera (Judith Bauer Stamper)

Rise and Shine, Mariko-Chan! (Chiyoko Tomioka)

Something From Nothing (Phoebe Gilman)

The Secret Birthday Message (Eric Carle)

The Teeny-Tiny Woman (Paul Galdone)

Ten, Nine, Eight (Molly Bang)

Uncle Nacho's Hat (Harriet Rohmer)

Wash and Dry (Judith Bauer Stamper)

We Were Tired of Living in a House (Liesel Moak Skorpen)

Wemberly Worried (Kevin Henkes)

Who Wears What (Judith Bauer Stamper)

A World of Families (Trish Holland)

As children demonstrate interest in other aspects of community life, the Dramatic Play area should change or be modified to address the changing roles, language, and mathematical experiences associated with each new topic. The charts that follow offer suggestions for integrating mathematical materials and books into four settings: a grocery store, a doctors' office, a shoe store, and a restaurant. There are many other possibilities, of course.

Materials

Grocery store

flyers, signs, coupons, and advertisements from local supermarkets

paper, cardboard, markers, and tape for making signs for different sections (e.g., meat, dairy) and labels for shelves

empty food containers

stick-on labels or price tags

number stamps and stamp pads

cash register

play money, checkbooks, credit cards

shopping list pads and/or receipt pads

balance scale

materials for a cake-decorating center if your local supermarket has one

Suggested Books

(Titles preceded by an asterisk are included in the Teaching Strategies Children's Book Collection.)

At the Supermarket (David Hautzig)

Each Orange Had 8 Slices (Paul Giganti, Jr.)

I Shop with My Daddy (Grace Maccarone)

Jelly Beans for Sale (Bruce McMillan)

Just Shopping With Mom (Mercer Mayer)

Lemonade for Sale (Bettina Ling)

Pigs Go to Market (Amy Axelrod)

Pigs Will Be Pigs: Fun with Math and Money (Amy Axelrod)

The Supermarket (Anne F. Rockwell)

Tommy at the Grocery Store (Bill Grossman)

Materials

Restaurant

cash register

plates, cups, silverware, napkins

order pads

menus or materials for children to make menus

play money, checkbooks, credit cards

wallets and purses

paper, cardboard, markers, and tape for making

signs, e.g., "Daily Specials" or "Pay here"

Suggested Books

(Titles preceded by an asterisk are included in the Teaching Strategies Children's Book Collection.)

A Chef (Douglas Florian)

Dim Sum for Everyone! (Grace Lin)

Dinner at the Panda Palace (Stephanie Calmenson)

Hi, Pizza Man (Virginia Walter)

In the Diner (Christine Loomis)

Marge's Diner (Gail Gibbons)

Miss Mabel's Table (Deborah Chandra)

One Pizza, One Penny (K. G. Hao)

Spaghetti and Meatballs for All (Marilyn Burns)

Materials

Shoe store

shoes of various sizes and styles	play money, checkbooks, credit cards
shoeboxes of various sizes	wallets and purses
ruler or foot measure	paper, cardboard, markers, and tape for making signs (e.g., *Men, Women, Children*)
order forms and receipt pads	
sticky labels or price tags	
cash register	

Suggested Books

Hello, Shoes! (Joan Blos)

My Best Shoes (Marilee Robin Burton)

New Shoes for Silvia (Johanna Hurwitz)

New Shoes, Red Shoes (Susan Rollings)

Shoes, Shoes, Shoes (Ann Morris)

Whose Shoe? (Margaret Miller)

Whose Shoes Are These? (Ron Roy)

Using Dramatic Play to Teach Mathematics

Teachers observe children engaged in dramatic play and then thoughtfully consider ways in which to promote their mathematics learning. Sometimes a teacher may let a child wrestle with a problem; at other times she may pose a question, model the use of a material or the way in which a problem is solved, or become a full-fledged player. Here are some examples of what teachers might say and do as they interact with children in the Dramatic Play area to promote mathematical skills and thinking:

Number and Operations

"Lunch is ready for you, Marla, Andre, and Keisha. How many places do you need at the table?"

"Let's see. I'm buying an apple for 3 cents and a pear for 2 cents. One, two, three (putting down 3 cents); one, two (putting down 2 cents). That's one, two, three, four, five. I owe you 5 cents."

"Your shoe store has a wonderful selection of shoes! Are there more shoes for children or for adults?"

"Yes, I may come to the birthday party. I'll need you to give me your address and directions to your home."

"You have four bracelets on your arm. If you shared two with a friend, how many would you still have?"

Geometry and Spatial Sense

"What shapes of cheese have you made? May I have a round one, please?"

"Where do you think we should put the baby's bed?"

"Apples, oranges, grapes, and pears are all fruits. Tell me another way that they are alike. What about their shapes?"

"How are the coffee can, the oatmeal box, and the roll of paper towels similar in shape?"

"How is the shape of an egg different from the shape of a ball?"

Measurement

"How do you know that this tablecloth is big enough to cover the table?"

"I'm not sure about what shoe size I wear. Will you help me find out?"

"I see you set the timer for 5 minutes. Is that how much longer the cake needs to bake?"

"Your baby's growing very fast! How much does she weigh now?"

"What time do you begin serving lunch? Hmmm, what size pizza should I get: large, medium, or small?"

Patterns (Algebra)

"Your baby's dress is like the flag: red, white; red, white; red…."

"I wonder why the rind on this watermelon has a pattern (dark green, light green, dark green, light green) and the other does not. What do you think?"

"You've chosen just the right beads to match your dress. Do you see a pattern? Tell me about it."

"There is a pattern on the sole of this shoe. How would you describe it?"

Data Analysis

"I see you're doing laundry. I usually sort the light-colored clothes from the dark-colored clothes. Does your mother do that?"

"Where does the cereal box go? Where does the dog food belong?"

"She wants shoes that do not have laces. Can you help her?"

"You've been busy measuring everyone. Would you like to make a chart showing how tall your classmates are?"

Mathematical Process Skills (Reasoning, Problem Solving, Communicating, Connecting, and Representing)

"What will you do first? What will you do next?"

"I wonder…"

"Tell me more about that."

"How did you figure that out?"

"Show me how you…"

"How is this like…?"

Observing Children's Progress

As you observe children engaged in dramatic play, look for these indications of mathematics development and learning:

- placing objects in one-to-one correspondence (e.g., putting one sock and one shoe on each foot of the doll, and setting the table)

- counting

- using ordinal numerals (e.g., to describe what to do first, second, third, and so on when cooking)

- reading or writing numbers (e.g., on recipes, addresses, or price tags)

- measuring (e.g., children's height and weight in the doctor's office; feet in the shoe store)

- comparing sizes (e.g., shoes or cereal boxes)

- sorting (e.g., groceries or clothing)

- using math terms (e.g., as *same–different, more–less, bigger–smaller, some–all, not*)

- using positional or directional terms (e.g., *near–far; in front of–in back of; on–off; on top of; under;* and *behind*)

- using time and relational words (e.g., *morning, afternoon, evening, tomorrow, yesterday, early, late, fast,* and slow)

- solving problems

- using pictures or symbols to represent something else (e.g., using checkers for pepperoni)

- talking about plans and ideas

Mathematics in the Art Area

The Art area is rich in opportunities for mathematics learning. Children explore size, shape, and spatial relationships as they use three-dimensional materials for sculpting and collage. They describe patterns in wallpaper samples and create their own patterns with stencils or paint and sponges. Representation, which is basic to art, is also fundamental to mathematics, which relies on symbols to represent concepts. Here are examples of how children's explorations in the Art area relate to the *The Creative Curriculum for Preschool* objectives for mathematics development and learning.

Examples of What a Child Might Do	Examples of Related Objectives for Development and Learning
Count five buttons for a play dough snowman and say, "My snowman's gonna wear one, two, three, four, five buttons."	Objective 20. Uses number concepts and operations a. Counts
Collect markers to put away and say, "Three markers don't have tops."	Objective 20. Uses number concepts and operations b. Quantifies
Bend a length of wire and say, "This looks like a *7*. I made a *7*."	Objective 20. Uses number concepts and operations c. Connects numerals with their quantities
Explain that, in a drawing, the sky is above the house and the tree is beside the house	Objective 21. Explores and describes spatial relationships and shapes a. Understands spatial relationships
Roll play dough into balls and say, "These are round. That's why they roll."	Objective 21. Explores and describes spatial relationships and shapes b. Understands shapes
Say that the roller makes wide lines on the paper and the marker makes thin lines	Objective 22. Compares and measures
Make a sponge print pattern of round, square; round, square; etc.	Objective 23. Demonstrates knowledge of patterns

Mathematics Materials for the Art Area

All of the items in a well-stocked Art area have possibilities for mathematical discoveries. The following materials and books may inspire additional mathematical explorations.

Materials

templates or stencils of geometric shapes

shape sponges

wallpaper and fabric samples

easel paper cut into a variety of shapes

rulers

pipe cleaners

brushes and/or rollers in two or more widths

thick and thin crayons

shape and numeral cookie cutters

printmaking materials (e.g., corks, spools, sponges, stamp pads)

modeling materials and tools

collage and construction materials (e.g., Styrofoam® packing sheets in assorted sizes)

geometric solids

everyday materials in the shape of geometric solids (e.g., spools, boxes, cardboard tubes, cone-shaped cups)

Suggested Books

(Titles preceded by an asterisk are included in the Teaching Strategies Children's Book Collection.)

Colors! ¡Colores!
(Jorge Luján and Piet Grobler)

Don't Lose It—Reuse It!
(Nancy Noel Williams)

Harold and the Purple Crayon
(Crockett Johnson)

I Spy Shapes in Art
(Lucy Micklethwait)

I Spy Two Eyes: Numbers in Art
(Lucy Micklethwait)

It Looked Like Spilt Milk
(Charles G. Shaw)

Mouse Paint (Ellen Stoll Walsh)

The Pot That Juan Built
(Nancy Andrews-Goebel)

Ten Black Dots (Donald Crews)

Using Art to Teach Mathematics

Your primary role in the Art area is to facilitate children's art explorations and creations. By observing children and listening to them talk about their work, teachers can decide whether and when to call children's attention to mathematical concepts. Here are examples of what you might say:

Number and Operations

"You punched many holes in your clay. Shall we count them?"

"Please put one paintbrush in each of the paint pots."

"Can you make a picture by using only three colors of paint?"

"You drew a picture of your family. Who are these two large persons? Who are the three small persons? How many persons are there altogether?"

Geometry and Spatial Sense

"I see triangles, circles, and rectangles in your picture."

"Can you make your play dough into the shape of a ball? What will happen if you flatten it into a pancake? Is the same amount of play dough in the ball and the pancake?"

"Tell me about your sculpture. How did you decide which shapes to use? How did you get the sphere to balance on top of the tower?"

"Tell me where you plan to place that piece on your collage."

Measurement

"You made long lines and short lines, and big circles and little circles."

"Will you use the thick paintbrush or the thin one for your picture?"

"Your snake is longer. Mine is shorter and fatter. What can I do to make mine as long as yours? How will we know when they are the same?"

"You drew the moon and stars in the sky above the house. It must be night. Tell me what's happening."

Patterns (Algebra)

"Red dot, blue dot; red dot, blue dot; red dot, blue dot; red dot, blue dot; red dot, blue dot. You made a pattern!"

"Look at the pattern that the truck tires made in the paint."

"I see you drew a pattern on your snake just like the one we saw in the photo. Can you read it?"

Data Analysis

"Do you have something on your collage that's the same as this? What do you have that's different from this?"

"You and Shakira both used the same yarn and cotton balls, but your pictures are quite different."

"Tell me why you drew this line down the middle of your paper and glued these things here. Are they alike in some way?"

Mathematical Process Skills (Reasoning, Problem Solving, Communicating, Connecting, and Representing)

"Can you draw some of the animals that we saw yesterday?"

"How did you make your play dough snake so long?"

"Tell me how you made that color of paint."

"Tell me about your picture."

"How did you decide…?"

"I wonder what would happen if you…"

Observing Children's Progress

As children create and explore in the Art area, look for these indications of mathematics development and learning:

- counting, recognizing, or writing numerals (e.g., printing numerals and then naming them, forming clay balls and counting them, drawing and labeling a picture of three friends)
- naming, drawing, or sculpting two- and three-dimensional shapes
- making patterns (e.g., color, shape, object)
- using measurement terms (e.g., *long, short, thin, thick, wide, narrow, taller, shorter*)
- sorting materials (e.g., making a collage of things that are red and things that are not red)
- using the terms *same* and *different*
- telling what they will be making and then painting or constructing it

Mathematics in the Library Area

In the Library area, children explore books and listen to or retell stories that highlight mathematical concepts. *My Little Sister Ate One Hare* (Bill Grossman) has a growing number pattern and repetitive, patterned text. Children enjoy hearing the story repeatedly, and, with picture props, teachers can intentionally call children's attention to the growing number pattern. When the book and props are left in the Library area, children can continue to use them to build oral language, literacy, and mathematical skills.

Books such as *Titch* (Pat Hutchins) help children learn about size differences. The Spot books (Eric Hill) invite children to use positional terms to answer *where* questions. *Mr. Gumpy's Outing* and many other books are filled with characters to be counted. Adding concept books such as Tana Hoban's *Let's Count* or *Shapes, Shapes, Shapes* to the Library area increases opportunities for children to learn about number and geometry. The Library area can nurture children's literacy and mathematics learning as well as broaden their understanding of the world. Here are examples of how children's explorations in the Library area relate to *The Creative Curriculum for Preschool* objectives for mathematics development and learning.

Examples of What a Child Might Do	Examples of Related Objectives for Development and Learning
Put one cap on each flannel board monkey	Objective 20. Uses number concepts and operations a. Counts
Hold up appropriate numbers of fingers while reciting "Five Little Monkeys"	Objective 20. Uses number concepts and operations b. Quantifies
Stack caps, put like colors together, and count the caps in each group while acting out *Caps for Sale* (Esphyr Slobodkina)	Objective 20. Uses number concepts and operations c. Connects numerals with their quantities
Say, "Spot is under the chair," and point to the dog in an illustration	Objective 21. Explores and describes spatial relationships and shapes a. Understands spatial relationships
Draw rectangles of different sizes after reading *Freight Train* (Donald Crews)	Objective 21. Explores and describes spatial relationships and shapes b. Understands shapes
Point to the caterpillar in an illustration and say, "That hungry caterpillar is getting bigger and bigger!"	Objective 22. Compares and measures

Examples of What a Child Might Do	Examples of Related Objectives for Development and Learning
Describe the patterns pictured in *Pattern Fish* (Trudy Harris) by saying, "I like this page. It has red, pink, red, pink, red, pink stripes on it."	Objective 23. Demonstrates knowledge of patterns

Mathematics Materials for the Library Area

The Library area in your classroom probably already contains books that can be used to talk about mathematical concepts with children. In fact, many picture books address several mathematical ideas. For example, in the book *Five Creatures* (Emily Jenkins), the child narrator counts the creatures that live in her house: three humans and two cats. She then groups and counts them in different ways: "three short and two tall," "three who can button buttons," "four who like to eat fish," and "two who like to eat mice."

The Library area should include nonfiction that reflects mathematical ideas as well as fiction that tells a good story and invites children to explore mathematical concepts. The following chart lists materials and a few of the many books that entice children to explore mathematics through literature.

Materials

felt props for recalling counting or number stories or rhymes

props for dramatizing or retelling stories that also address mathematical concepts (e.g., three sizes of bowls and chairs for acting out *The Three Bears;* hats for *Caps for Sale;* small plastic animals and a mitten for *The Mitten*)

paper and writing/drawing tools so that children can make their own representations of a story or make number/counting books

story tapes or CDs that help children understand mathematical concepts

charts of counting/number rhymes or chants (e.g., *Two Little Blackbirds Sitting on a Hill*)

class-made books (e.g., counting books, books of patterns children have created)

Suggested Books

(Titles preceded by an asterisk are included in the Teaching Strategies Children's Book Collection.)

Biggest, Strongest, Fastest (Steve Jenkins)

Caps for Sale (Esphyr Slobodkina)

Chicka Chicka 1 2 3 (Bill Martin, Jr., Michael Sampson, Lois Ehlert)

Come Back, Hannah! (Marisabina Russo)

Cook-a-Doodle-Doo (Janet Stevens and Susan Stevens Crummel)

Counting Crocodiles (Judy Sierra)

Cubes, Cones, Cylinders, and Spheres (Tana Hoban)

Do You See a Mouse? (Bernard Waber)

A Dozen Ducklings Lost and Found (Harriet Ziefert)

Five Creatures (Emily Jenkins)

Five Little Monkeys Wash the Car (Eileen Christelow)

Freight Train (Donald Crews)

Inside Mouse, Outside Mouse (Lindsay Barrett George)

Is It Larger? Is It Smaller? (Tana Hoban)

The Jacket I Wear in the Snow (Shirley Neitzel)

Lemons Are Not Red (Laura Seegar)

Lots and Lots of Zebra Stripes (Stephen R. Swinburne)

The Mitten (Jan Brett)

Mrs. McTats and Her Houseful of Cats (Alyssa Satin Capucilli)

One for Me, One for You (C. C. Cameron)

One Lighthouse, One Moon (Anita Lobel)

One More Bunny; Adding from One to Ten (Rick Walton)

A Pair of Socks (Stuart J. Murphy)

Pattern Fish (Trudy Harris)

Rosie's Walk (Pat Hutchins)

Shrinking Mouse (Pat Hutchins)

Ten Go Tango (Arthur Dorros)

Ten Mice for Tet! (Pegi Deitz Shea and Cynthia Weill)

Ten Puppies (Lynn Reiser)

The Relatives Came (Cynthia Rylant)

The Teeny-Tiny Woman (Paul Galdone)

Uno, Dos, Tres = One, Two, Three (Pat Mora)

We're Going on a Picnic (Pat Hutchins)

When I Was Little: A Four-Year-Old's Memoir of Her Youth (Jamie Lee Curtis)

Where Is the Green Sheep? (Mem Fox and Judy Horacek)

Using the Library Area to Teach Mathematics

The primary reason for setting up the Library area is to encourage children to enjoy and explore books. Books also offer teachers numerous opportunities for presenting mathematical ideas to children. In the same way that you teach children about letters, rhyme, and print, you can call their attention to concepts of number, size, shape, space, pattern, and sequence. Here are some examples of questions and comments you might use as you share books with children:

Number and Operations

"Look at all the mice. I've never seen so many! How many do you think there are?"

"Do you remember which billy goat crossed the bridge first (second, third)?"

"Are there more red sheep or more blue sheep? How do you know?"

Geometry and Spatial Sense

"What shapes do you see? How do you know that they are triangles?"

"Do you remember where Rosie the hen walked after she went across the yard, around the pond, and over the haystack?"

"Can you find the mouse? Where is he?"

Measurement

"Do you think all of the animals can fit into the mitten? Why? How large do think the mitten will get?"

"That pig is so funny! Cook-a-Doodle-Doo told him to measure the flour, so he measured it with a ruler. What should the pig have used to measure the flour for the cake?"

"Can you tell me some of the things Jesse wore in the morning? What did he wear at noon and at night?"

Patterns (Algebra)

"If the little girl in the story ate one hare, two snakes, and three ants, how many of the next animal do you think she will eat?"

"Do you remember what the dog, cat, and goose told the Little Red Hen each time she asked for help? Read it with me."

"Now that you know the pattern, read with me. 'Polar Bear, Polar Bear, what do you hear? I hear a…'"

Data Analysis

"You chose books about animals. Do you want to find all the books about animals and put them on this shelf?"

"Some of you like this version of *The Three Bears*, and some of you like the version that Mr. Alvarez is holding. If you like this one, sit by me. If you prefer the other version, sit by Mr. Alvarez. Which book do most of you like best?"

"What's different about these two versions of *The Three Bears*?"

Mathematical Process Skills (Reasoning, Problem Solving, Communicating, Connecting, and Representing)

"I wonder why... What do you think?"

"Have you ever been told to share your cookies? How can the children in the story share their cookies so everyone has the same number?"

"Can you think of another way for the peddler to get his caps back?"

"Would you like to draw a picture of that?"

Observing Children's Progress

As you observe and share books with children in the Library area, look for these indications of mathematics development and learning:

- counting, using one-to-one correspondence, or identifying numerals
- telling who's first, second, or last
- recalling the sequence of events in a story
- identifying quantity or using terms such as *some, all, more, less*
- recognizing patterns in a story or the language of the text
- naming or describing shapes
- using positional words such as *over, under, in front of, next to, behind*
- using comparative terms such as *big, bigger, biggest; faster, slower; longer, longest*
- talking about how things are the same or different
- suggesting solutions to problems presented in stories

Mathematics in the Discovery Area

The Discovery area has materials that spark children's curiosity and wonder. Children handle and examine objects, experiment, and make discoveries. As they explore, children can use mathematical thinking to help them focus their observations, organize their thoughts, and record their findings.

Mathematics is closely related to science and technology. In these content areas, children observe, count, sort and classify, compare objects, measure, discover patterns, and collect data. The mathematical process skills—reasoning, problem-solving, communicating, connecting, and representing—are also needed by scientists. In the Discovery area, teachers help children develop their observation and reasoning skills as they use their senses to explore. Here are examples of how children's explorations in the Discovery area relate to *The Creative Curriculum for Preschool* objectives for mathematics development and learning.

Examples of What a Child Might Do	Examples of Related Objectives for Development and Learning
Put each rock from a collection in a separate section of an egg carton	Objective 20. Uses number concepts and operations a. Counts
Look in the rabbit cage and say, "There are three carrots for her to eat today."	Objective 20. Uses number concepts and operations b. Quantifies
Put two pinches of fish food in the tank after looking at the sign above the tank that says, "Only use 2 pinches."	Objective 20. Uses number concepts and operations c. Connects numerals with their quantities
Look for the gerbil and say, "The gerbil is hiding inside the tube."	Objective 21. Explores and describes spatial relationships and shapes a. Understands spatial relationships
Use an eyedropper to drop colored water on paper and say, "It makes a water circle on the paper when I squeeze it."	Objective 21. Explores and describes spatial relationships and shapes b. Understands shapes
Pick up a pumpkin and say, "This pumpkin is bigger and heavier than that one."	Objective 22. Compares and measures
Describe the striped pattern of a shell	Objective 23. Demonstrates knowledge of patterns

Mathematics Materials for the Discovery Area

Common Discovery area equipment such as magnifying glasses, magnets, prisms, balance scales, eyedroppers, thermometers, tweezers, and clear plastic cups are also useful for mathematics explorations because children use them to observe, measure, count, and sort. Writing and graphing materials enable children to represent and record information. For example, they might draw a picture each day of the changes that occur in a bean seed resting on a wet paper towel, or they might put a tally mark next to the picture of the food the gerbil eats first every day.

The following chart lists books and materials that support mathematical experiences. You can add other items related to your current topic of study to help children see the connections between mathematics, science, and technology.

Materials

collections of natural materials for sorting (e.g., shells, leaves, seeds, soil, rocks)

sorting trays, bowls, or other containers (e.g., muffin tins, ice cube trays, clean egg cartons)

standard measuring tools (e.g., rulers, tape measures, liquid and dry measuring cups, balance scale, timers, calendar)

nonstandard measuring tools (e.g., string, paper clips, craft sticks)

writing materials to record observations and data

graphs and charts, including sequencing charts (e.g., step-by-step instructions for planting seeds)

Suggested Books

(Titles preceded by an asterisk are included in the Teaching Strategies Children's Book Collection.)

The Adventures of Gary & Harry (Lisa Matsumoto)

Apples and Pumpkins (Anne Rockwell)

Fish Eyes: A Book You Can Count On (Lois Ehlert)

Growing Trees (Judith Bauer Stamper)

The Icky Bug Counting Book (Jerry Pallotta)

It's Fall, It's Summer, It's Spring, It's Winter (four books by Linda Glaser)

Lots and Lots of Zebra Stripes: Patterns in Nature (Stephen R. Swinburne)

One Bean (Anne Rockwell)

One Child, One Seed: A South African Counting Book (Kathryn Cave)

One Guinea Pig Is Not Enough (Kate Duke)

Pablo's Tree (Pat Mora)

Pumpkin, Pumpkin (Anne Titherington)

Red Leaf, Yellow Leaf (Lois Ehlert)

Sam Helps Recycle (Judith Bauer Stamper)

Suggested Books

Seeds! Seeds! Seeds! (Nancy Elizabeth Wallace and Marshal Cavendish)

Sense Suspense: A Guessing Game for the Senses (Bruce McMillan)

The Surprise Garden (Zoe Hall)

Ten Flashing Fireflies (Philemon Sturges)

Ten Seeds (Ruth Brown)

*A Tree Is For… (Judith Bauer Stamper)

*Trees Count (Trish Holland)

Two Bad Ants (Chris Van Allsburg)

*Who Lives in Trees? (Trish Holland)

*When the Monkeys Came Back (Kristine Franklin)

Using the Discovery Area to Teach Mathematics

The Discovery area invites children to observe, explore, and investigate natural materials. In the Discovery area, they sort classify, compare, and measure. By supporting children's investigations in the Discovery area, you also promote their mathematics learning, especially their process skills: reasoning, problem solving, communicating, connecting, and representing. Your most effective interactions may begin with "I wonder why…" or "What would happen if…?" The following questions and comments may be useful in drawing children's attention to the mathematics involved in their explorations. Encouraging children to ask questions is even more important than asking questions, yourself.

Number and Operations

"These X-rays are very interesting. How many ribs did you count?"

"Yes, you may add the leaves you found on the playground to our collection. How many do you have in your hand?"

"How many more small rocks are there than large rocks? How do you know? Show me."

Geometry and Spatial Sense

"I wonder why the balls roll down the ramp but the boxes don't. What do you think?"

"Where is the gerbil hiding today?"

"Hmm, what happens…?"

Measurement

"Do you want to keep track of how tall your plant grows? Now it's short. We could put one of these connecting cubes next to it, because that's how tall it is. When it gets as tall as two cubes, you can add another one."

"This side of the balance scale went down when you put the rock on it. I wonder how many acorns you'd have to add to the other side to make it level. Would you like to find out?"

"If you put another block under the ramp, do you think the ball will roll faster or at the same speed?"

"Wow! The gak is getting longer and longer and thinner and thinner!"

Patterns (Algebra)

"How are these shells alike? How are they different?"

"You chose different kinds of rocks. Tell me about them."

"Did you notice the pattern on this leaf? How would you describe it? Would you like to make a rubbing of it?"

Data Analysis

"How could you sort all the things you found in the soil? Are there more rocks or more twigs? How can you tell without counting?"

"Why do these belong together?"

"Can you find another feather that would go in this group? What name could you give to this group?"

"What does your graph tell you?"

Mathematical Process Skills (Reasoning, Problem Solving, Communicating, Connecting, and Representing)

"Tell me why you think that."

"Can you think of a way to…?"

"Tell me what you're working on."

"Can you think of another time when…?"

"Would you like to draw a picture or make a sign about that?"

Observing Children's Progress

As children explore in the Discovery area, look for these indications of mathematics development and learning:

- counting
- using terms such as *some, all, more, less*
- identifying, describing, copying, or creating patterns
- describing shapes and their properties
- using positional words (e.g., *over, under, in front of, next to, behind*)
- measuring with standard and nonstandard tools
- using terms related to weight such as *heavy, heavier, light, lighter*
- using terms related to time (e.g., *days, minutes, faster, slower*)
- describing how things are the same and different
- contributing to or creating a chart or graph
- talking about their investigations
- representing their thinking and learning (e.g., creating a model, drawing a picture, dictating, or writing)

Mathematics in the Sand and Water Area

The soothing properties of sand and water make this one of the children's favorite areas. Here, children have many opportunities informally to explore mathematical concepts, particularly measurement. As they fill and empty various sizes and shapes of containers, children estimate, count, and learn about weight, volume, and capacity. Adding water to sand along with molds and other tools and props enables children to explore shapes, patterns, and other dimensions of mathematics. Here are examples of how children's explorations in the Sand and Water area relate to *The Creative Curriculum for Preschool* objectives for mathematics development and learning.

Examples of What a Child Might Do	Examples of Related Objectives for Development and Learning
Put one bear in each boat and say, "Each bear has a boat to drive."	Objective 20. Uses number concepts and operations a. Counts
Pour four scoops of sand into a pail when prompted	Objective 20. Uses number concepts and operations b. Quantifies
Catch six plastic fish to put in the container labeled *6*	Objective 20. Uses number concepts and operations c. Connects numerals with their quantities
Say, "My truck is at the top of the hill, and yours is at the bottom."	Objective 21. Explores and describes spatial relationships and shapes a. Understands spatial relationships
Say, "The square blower makes round bubbles."	Objective 21. Explores and describes spatial relationships and shapes b. Understands shapes
Sift sand to find shells and then line them up from largest to smallest	Objective 22. Compares and measures
Create a pattern in the sand by using a rake and say, "Look, the sand is high and low, high and low."	Objective 23. Demonstrates knowledge of patterns

Mathematics Materials for the Sand and Water Area

The addition of well-chosen materials and books can enhance mathematics learning experiences. The materials listed in the chart below are not meant to be added all at once. Choose props on the basis of your current mathematical focus or study topic.

Materials

Sand

rakes and large combs for creating patterns

collections for sorting, counting, weighing (e.g., shells, rocks, other natural materials)

sorting and counting trays (e.g., muffin tins, ice cube trays, or clean egg cartons)

standard and nonstandard measuring tools (e.g., craft sticks, links)

molds of various shapes and sizes (e.g., cube, cone, cylinder)

cookie cutters (e.g., numeral and shape)

balance scale

props related to a current topic of study

Water

magnetic fishing pole and fish (for counting and sorting or labeled with numerals)

containers of various dimensions (e.g., tall, short, narrow, wide)

containers with holes punched in sides and/or bottom

clear plastic liquid measuring cups

boats or small trays that will serve as boats

collections of objects (e.g., plastic animals or people, and materials such as corks for exploring the concepts of sinking and floating)

tubing and funnels, cooking baster

strainers of various sizes

vinyl graph

plastic sorting bowls or trays

Suggested Books

(Titles preceded by an asterisk are included in the Teaching Strategies Children's Book Collection.)

Drip Drop (Sarah Weeks)

Five Little Ducks (Ian Beck)

Is This a House for Hermit Crab? (Megan McDonald)

Math in the Bath (Sara Atherlay)

One Less Fish (Kim Michelle Toft)

Sea Shapes (Suse MacDonald)

Sea Sums (Joy Hulme)

Splash (Ann Jonas)

Underwater Counting (Jerry Pallota)

Water (Frank Asch)

Water, Water (Eloise Greenfield)

What Lives in a Shell? (Kathleen Weidner Zoehfeld)

Who Sank the Boat? (Pamela Allen)

Using Sand and Water to Teach Mathematics

Teachers can take advantage of children's enjoyment of sand and water to introduce the language of mathematics and to teach many concepts and skills. Encourage children to talk about and explain what they are doing, e.g., "Tell me how you made this tunnel." Supply words, e.g., "It's full. Now it's half-full. Now it's empty." Describe what children are doing, e.g., "You are splashing water over the side of the water table." Wonder aloud, e.g., "Hmmm, I wonder whether there is a way to make the water wheel turn faster. What do you think?" Ask questions, e.g., "Which one is heavier? Why do you think that is?"

Some children enjoy using sand and water for pretend purposes, e.g., "I added sugar, so now it's lemonade." You can support their play through your responses and expression of interest. Because you recognize that free exploration is valuable for children, you will want to observe for a while before stepping in to promote their understanding of mathematical concepts and vocabulary.

Questions and comments can help focus children's attention on the mathematics involved in sand and water play, but be mindful that questioning can also interrupt children's thinking and distract from their learning. Always begin by observing. Then thoughtfully determine whether, when, and how you should step in.

Number and Operations

"How many bears did you put in your boat before it sank?"

"You found lots of rocks in the sand. I see you put two in each section of the muffin tin. How many do you have altogether?"

"How many scoops of sand do you think you'll need to fill this bowl? How can you check your estimate?"

"How many fish did you catch?"

Geometry and Spatial Sense

"How did you get your hill so smooth and round on the top? Can you make a hill that's pointed on the top?"

"What container do you think Derek used to make his castle? How can you find out?"

"Which container did **not** make this shape? How do you know?"

Measurement

"I wonder how much sand you would need to make a hill big enough to hide this truck."

"Do you think this bottle holds more water than the bowl? Why? How could you check to be sure?"

"If you try to pour the sand back into the bowl, do you think it will fit? How could you find out?"

"Which bowl is heavier, the one with wet sand or dry sand? How could you find out?"

"Why is one bowl of sand heavier than the other?"

Patterns (Algebra)

"Look at the tire tracks! Which vehicle made these? How do you know?"

"I see that you used tiles to make a path around your hill. Tell me about the pattern you created."

"You discovered a lot of shells in the sand. Can you read the pattern on this one?"

Data Analysis

"Tell me why you decided to put the stick, boat, and Styrofoam® peanut in this basket and the key, rock, and screw in this basket?"

"How are these shells alike? How are they different?"

"Can you think of a way to organize our water props so everyone can find what he or she needs?"

Mathematical Process Skills (Reasoning, Problem Solving, Communicating, Connecting, and Representing)

"Tell me why you think…"

"The funnel is missing. What else could you use to get the sand through the narrow neck of the bottle?"

"Tell the class what you discovered!"

"When you pour water on the sand, the sand washes away. That reminds me of what happened to the hill on our playground.

"Would you like to record your recipe for mud pies in the notebook? That way, you can remember exactly how you made it."

Observing Children's Progress

As children explore sand and water, look for these indications of mathematics development and learning:

- estimating and counting (e.g., the number of scoops to fill a pail)

- comparing capacity (e.g., using terms like *some, all, more, the same amount, less, too much, not enough, left over*)

- recognizing and/or creating patterns (e.g., using sand combs or making impressions in the sand)

- comparing sizes (e.g., *tall, taller, tallest; wide, wider, widest; highest, lowest; thick, thin; wide, narrow; shallow, deep*)

- comparing mass (e.g., *heavier, lighter*) and speed (*fast, faster, fastest; slow, slower, slowest*)

- using nonstandard measurements (e.g., tubful, bowlful)

- sorting and classifying collections of objects

- describing shapes (e.g., *round, curved, straight*)

- using positional terms (e.g., *around, on top of, over, under, through*)

Mathematics in the Music and Movement Area

Music and movement activities can enhance children's understanding of mathematical concepts. As children clap and dance to the beat of the music, they experience patterns physically. Moving to the tempo, or speed, of the music enables them to experience time, a measurement concept, firsthand. Children explore geometrical and spatial concepts when they transform their bodies into a ball and when they move forward and backward, around and through, back and forth, or up and down. Counting is reinforced by singing songs such as "Five Little Ducks" or "The Ants Go Marching." Here are examples of how children's explorations in the Music and Movement area relate to *The Creative Curriculum for Preschool* objectives for mathematics development and learning.

Examples of What a Child Might Do	Examples of Related Objectives for Development and Learning
Sing counting rhymes such as "One, Two, Three, Four, Five" ("Once I Caught a Fish Alive")	Objective 20. Uses number concepts and operations a. Counts
Point to an instrument and say, "That cello has four pegs."	Objective 20. Uses number concepts and operations b. Quantifies
Hold up appropriate numbers of fingers when singing a counting song	Objective 20. Uses number concepts and operations c. Connects numerals with their quantities
Respond to directional words, such as *forward*, *backward*, *up*, and *down*	Objective 21. Explores and describes spatial relationships and shapes a. Understands spatial relationships
March in a circle and say, "We're marching around in a parade!"	Objective 21. Explores and describes spatial relationships and shapes b. Understands shapes
Play a xylophone loudly, softly, and very softly, and say, "When I touch it like this, it's the quietest."	Objective 22. Compares and measures
Follow the teacher's lead: stamp, clap, clap; stamp, clap, clap; etc.	Objective 23. Demonstrates knowledge of patterns

Mathematics Materials for the Music and Movement Area

You can support children's mathematics development and learning in the Music and Movement area by offering a variety of musical instruments for them to explore and experiment with and by providing enough space for movement activities. The following chart suggests materials and books related to mathematics.

Materials

tapes or CDs of counting and shape songs

picture and word charts for counting songs

props related to favorite counting songs and chants (e.g., felt ducks for *Five Little Ducks*)

shakers that make distinctive sounds (e.g., cans or boxes filled with materials such as bottle caps, pebbles, or sand)

materials that encourage children to explore, copy, or create patterns (e.g., cards illustrating actions such as clapping, stamping, and tapping)

Suggested Books

(Titles preceded by an asterisk are included in the Teaching Strategies Children's Book Collection.)

Abiyoyo (Pete Seeger)

The Ants Go Marching One by One (Richard Bernal)

The Aunts Go Marching (Maurie Jo Manning)

Five Little Ducks: An Old Rhyme (Pamela Paparone)

Five Little Monkeys Jumping on the Bed (Eileen Christelow)

Max Found Two Sticks (Brian Pinkney)

Neighborhood Song (Trish Holland)

Over in the Meadow (versions by Ezra Jack Keats and Olive A. Wadsworth)

Roll Over! A Counting Song (Merle Peek)

Shape Space (Cathryn Falwell)

She'll be Coming 'Round the Mountain (Philemon Sturges)

Ten Go Tango (Arthur Dorros)

Ten in the Bed: A Counting Book (David Ellwand)

This Old Man (Carol Jones)

Using Music and Movement to Teach Mathematics

In many preschool classrooms, music and movement experiences typically occur during large-group times. Children need additional time to explore musical instruments independently and to experiment with ways to move their bodies and navigate space. This helps them gain a deeper understanding of mathematical concepts. As you observe children in action, you will be able to determine when and how to interact, whether it is to introduce new vocabulary, reinforce an idea, or ask a question to encourage or clarify a child's thinking. Here are examples of what you might say and ask:

Number and Operations

"One, two, three, four, five. You hopped five times."

"Last time, the ants went marching three by three. How many will march together this time? Show me."

"If three monkeys were jumping on the bed and one fell off, how many would be left on the bed?"

Geometry and Spatial Sense

"You're waving the streamer above your head? Can you make it go behind you? Now wave it beside you."

"You're marching around in a circle. Do you think you could march in a triangle?"

"Can you dance forward?...backward?...sideways?"

Measurement

"You played some very fast beats. How will it sound if you play the drum slowly?"

"Can you march low? How about high on your toes?"

"Some streamers are long; some are short. Which would you like?"

Patterns (Algebra)

"I hear your drum pattern. It sounds like DA, da, da; loud, soft, soft. Can you do that again?"

"Let's see if I can make the same pattern that you did. I think it was one, two, three; one, two, three..."

"Follow Leo! Clap front, clap back, then shake, shake, shake; clap front, clap back, then shake, shake, shake..."

Data Analysis

"Sonya wants to know what everyone's favorite song is. How can we find out?"

"Why did you put the cymbals, triangle, and bells together in a group?"

"Some of you have red streamers, and some of you have streamers that are not red."

"Without counting, how can we figure out which group has more?"

Mathematical Process Skills (Reasoning, Problem Solving, Communicating, Connecting, and Representing)

"Why does the smallest bar on the xylophone makes the highest sound?"

"Since you can't find the finger cymbals, can you think of another instrument that would be good to represent the sound of a mouse scurrying across the floor?"

"You're playing that drum slowly and loudly. It reminds me of how an elephant walks heavily like this."

"You made up new words to that song. Would you like to record it?"

Observing Children's Progress

As children explore music and movement, look for these indications of mathematics development and learning:

- counting while singing
- making predictions or estimating (e.g., how many baby steps it takes to walk from one place to another)
- making sound or movement patterns
- responding to or using directional or positional vocabulary (e.g., *forward–backward, high–low, up–down, around,* and through) to describe their motions
- describing rates of movement (e.g., *fast* or *slow*)
- using the terms *same* and *different* to compare sounds

Mathematics in the Cooking Area

Cooking provides children with opportunities to develop and use mathematical skills in meaningful ways. Through cooking, children are able to see the connection between mathematics and everyday life experiences. Recipes involve measuring, counting, and following a sequence of steps. Working with fruits and vegetables, for example in preparing fruit kabobs or vegetable soup, provides opportunities to explore shape, size, and pattern. Children use mathematical process skills as they attempt to explain why a recipe did not turn out as planned or as they try to determine how to divide a snack equally among a group. Of course, tasting makes learning mathematics even more fun! Here are examples of how children's explorations in the Cooking area relate to *The Creative Curriculum for Preschool* objectives for mathematics development and learning.

Examples of What a Child Might Do	Examples of Related Objectives for Development and Learning
Put one piece of cheese on each of three crackers	Objective 20. Uses number concepts and operations a. Counts
Take two hard-boiled eggs when prompted, "Choose two eggs to peel."	Objective 20. Uses number concepts and operations b. Quantifies
Point to 5 on the trail mix recipe chart and then count out five raisins	Objective 20. Uses number concepts and operations c. Connects numerals with their quantities
Say that the seeds are on the outside of the strawberry, not the inside	Objective 21. Explores and describes spatial relationships and shapes a. Understands spatial relationships
Use shape cutters to cut sandwiches and say, "I'm eating a star for lunch today!"	Objective 21. Explores and describes spatial relationships and shapes b. Understands shapes
Set a timer and say, "The muffins will be ready when the timer beeps in 10 minutes."	Objective 22. Compares and measures
Makes a patterned fruit kabob: apple slice, strawberry, banana slice; apple slice, etc.	Objective 23. Demonstrates knowledge of patterns

Mathematics Materials for the Cooking Area

Many standard cooking utensils, such as measuring spoons and cups, are also math tools. Much of the mathematics-related equipment listed in the chart below may already be in your Cooking area. Recipe charts, recipe cards, and class-made cookbooks are useful for promoting mathematical skills. You will find some simple recipes in *The Creative Curriculum for Preschool, Volume 2, Interest Areas*; *Come Cook With Me!* (included in the Teaching Strategies Children's Book Collection); and selected *Teaching Strategies Intentional Teaching Cards*.

Materials

picture/word recipes and charts

graduated measuring cups and spoons

clear measuring cup for liquids, marked ¼ cup, ½ cup, 4 oz., etc.

cookie cutters in geometric shapes

timer

candy thermometer

ruler

food pyramid materials for children (U. S. Dept. of Agriculture)

class-made graphs showing, for example, children's favorite kind of apples or what they like on celery

Suggested Books

(Titles preceded by an asterisk are included in the Teaching Strategies Children's Book Collection.)

10 for Dinner (Jo Ellen Bogart)

Bread, Bread, Bread (Ann Morris)

Cook-a-Doodle-Doo (Janet Stevens and Susan Stevens Crummel)

*The Doorbell Rang (Pat Hutchins)

Eating Fractions (Bruce McMillan)

Feast for 10 (Cathryn Falwell)

Growing Vegetable Soup (Lois Ehlert)

*Jalapeño Bagels (Natasha Wing)

Let's Eat! (Ana Zamorano)

*The Little Red Hen (Bonnie Dobkin)

The Little Red Hen Makes a Pizza (Philemon Sturges)

Magda's Tortillas (Becky Chavarria-Chairez)

Pancakes for Breakfast (Tomi DePaola)

*Peeny Butter Fudge (Toni Morrison and Slade Morrison)

Pretend Soup and Other Real Recipes: A Cookbook for Preschoolers and Up (Molly Katzen and Ann Henderson)

*Rice Is Nice (Nancy Noel Williams)

Round Is a Pancake (Joan Sullivan Baranski)

Seaweed Soup (Stuart J. Murphy)

Today Is Monday (Eric Carle)

*Too Many Tamales (Gary Soto)

Two Eggs, Please (Sarah Weeks)

Using Cooking to Teach Mathematics

Mathematics, especially number and measurement concepts, can be taught through cooking experiences. Children learn more when they do more. Plan experiences that include the use of picture and word recipes and encourage children to do their own measuring, counting, pouring, and mixing.

As you interact with children in the Cooking area, talk with them about similarities and differences. For example, have them compare the size and taste of oranges, tangerines, satsumas, and clementines. Call attention to the shapes of fruits and vegetables and the patterns that occur naturally in foods. Invite children to predict how many apples it will take to make a cup of applesauce or half a cup of apple juice. Then let them test their predictions. Here are examples of what you might say and ask to promote mathematics learning:

Number and Operations

"How many seeds did you find in your apple?"

"How many tablespoons of flour does the recipe call for? Count aloud as you add each one."

"Each person will need a cup for juice and a bowl for snack mix. How many cups will we need altogether?"

"How many strawberries do you think are in this basket?"

Geometry and Spatial Sense

"If we slice the carrot crosswise, what shape do you think the slices will be?"

"How will you cut your cheese so that it fits the cracker?"

"I'm thinking of a fruit that is smooth and round like a ball. Can you guess which one it is?"

"A slice of pizza has three sides and three points. What shape is the pizza slice?"

Measurement

"We need a bowl that will hold the batter for everyone's muffins. Can you find a bowl that will be big enough?"

"Fill each cup so that it is half full."

"We need to set the timer for 15 minutes. Will you please do that?"

"Which pitcher will hold more juice?"

Patterns (Algebra)

"Tell me about the pattern you see on the watermelon rind."

"You made a pattern with your raisins and pumpkin seeds."

"Even the mixing bowl has a pattern on the outside. Let's read it!"

"I see you have arranged the crackers in a pattern on the tray. I see a row of round crackers and then a row of square crackers, a row of round cracker and then a row of squares. If there were still some space, what shape would you put next?"

Data Analysis

"Some of you made blueberry muffins, and some of you made banana muffins. Without counting, how can we tell of which kind we made the most?"

"Let's look at our snack chart for today. Did more people have apple juice or orange juice?"

"Why did you put these two fruits in the same group? How are they the same?"

"To what food group do you think tortillas belong? What about cheese?"

Mathematical Process Skills (Reasoning, Problem Solving, Communicating, Connecting, and Representing)

"Now that the juice is frozen, it is taller than the cup. Why do you think that is?"

"The gelatin is still warm. I don't know if it will be ready for lunch. What should we do?"

"Crystal, why are you adding more flour to your dough?"

"This popcorn smells so good! Do you remember what happened when the children in the story we read popped corn?"

"You're enjoying your trail mix. Would you like to write the recipe so you can remember all of the ingredients you used?"

Observing Children's Progress

As children participate in cooking experiences or prepare snack, look for these indications of mathematics development and learning:

- using numbers (e.g., counting, reading and writing numerals, showing quantity)
- using one-to-one correspondence (e.g., putting one liner in each section of a muffin tin)
- recognizing, copying, or creating patterns
- naming, describing, or making shapes
- using measurement terms or tools (e.g., setting the timer for 7 minutes or saying, "This is the coldest thing I've ever tasted!")
- telling how items are the same and/or different
- contributing to or creating a graph
- making a sign or recipe with pictures
- explaining or demonstrating food preparation
- making connections among home, school, and community experiences
- solving a problem (e.g., dough is too sticky or too dry; dividing a snack equally among children)
- explaining reasoning (e.g., why he measured the pumpkin with a string instead of a block)

Mathematics in the Computer Area

By using computers, children can experience mathematics in new or different ways. They can create a character that has a specified number of body parts; they can change the size, position, or location of an image on screen; and they can create three-dimensional shapes. Children also can use the computer to practice skills, represent their ideas, or investigate topics such as the mole that has created long mounds in the play yard.

Discovery-based computer programs are ideal for promoting mathematical thinking while kindling children's imaginations and fostering creativity. Children solve problems such as figuring out how to transform an object; create patterns; and experiment with size, shape, color, number, and space. Here are examples of how children's explorations in the computer area relate to *The Creative Curriculum for Preschool* objectives for mathematics development and learning.

Examples of What a Child Might Do	Examples of Related Objectives for Development and Learning
Give every stuffed dog one bone and say, "Each dog gets one!"	Objective 20. Uses number concepts and operations a. Counts
Click the computer mouse to give a screen character more acorns and explain, "I'm giving the squirrel more nuts to fill up the tree hole."	Objective 20. Uses number concepts and operations b. Quantifies
Count images on the screen and select the corresponding numeral	Objective 20. Uses number concepts and operations c. Connects numerals with their quantities
Use the ↑ key to move the cursor up and the ↓ key to move it down	Objective 21. Explores and describes spatial relationships and shapes a. Understands spatial relationships
Select all of the four-sided figures from a group of shapes	Objective 21. Explores and describes spatial relationships and shapes b. Understands shapes
Select the shoes that fit a character in *Millie's Math House*	Objective 22. Compares and measures
Make a patterned drawing on the computer and say, "See my pattern? It has snowflake, circle; snowflake, circle; snowflake, circle…"	Objective 23. Demonstrates knowledge of patterns

Mathematics Materials for the Computer Area

The arrangement of the Computer area affects the way children use it. If you cluster computers together and place two chairs at each computer, children are likely to share their discoveries and assist one another. Learning is enhanced when children interact and communicate.

Choosing appropriate software to enhance mathematics learning can be challenging. Software that is open-ended and engages children in thinking, problem solving, and creating supports the development of mathematical process skills and promotes children's overall cognitive development. The computer programs listed in the following chart are interactive and encourage children to explore a variety of mathematical concepts and skills.

Software suggestions

Clifford the Big Red Dog™ Thinking Adventures (Scholastic)

Curious George Downtown Adventure (Knowledge Adventure)

Does It Belong? (Navarre)

Fredi Fish 5: The Case of the Creature of Coral Cove (Humongous Entertainment)

How Many Bugs in a Box? (Simon & Schuster Interactive)

KidPix® (The Learning Company)

Millie's Math House (Edmark/Riverdeep)

Little Bill Thinks Big (Scholastic)

Ollo and the Sunny Valley Fair (Plaid Banana Entertainment)

Putt-Putt: Pep's Birthday Surprise (Atari)

Putt-Putt Joins the Circus (Atari)

Stuart Little: His Adventures in Numberland (The Learning Company)

Thinkin' Things (Edmark/Riverdeep)

Thomas and Friends: Trouble on the Tracks (Hasbro Interactive)

The interactive opportunities that software programs offer can be increased when the controls are designed for young children. The standard mouse and keyboard (with over 100 keys) are not child friendly. Other options are available at computer supply stores and through catalogs that provide better ways to control what happens on the screen. Here are some ideas:

Mouse alternatives

- touch screen—This clear screen fits over the monitor. Children touch the screen instead of clicking the mouse.

- trackball—A large "upside-down" mouse. Children move the ball to move the pointer on the screen. A separate button is clicked to make a choice.

- squeezable mice—Instead of using one finger to click, smaller mice are available that children squeeze rather than tap.

Keyboard alternatives

- keyboards with larger, fewer, more colorful keys
- keyboards with letter keys arranged in alphabetical order so that children can find particular letters more easily

Software for young children often requires the use of just a few keys. Consider highlighting the important ones with stickers, Velcro®, or raised dots.

Using Computers to Teach Mathematics

Your guidance, enthusiasm, and responsiveness foster children's computer learning. As in the other areas, you can give encouragement, ask open-ended questions, provide assistance, and pose problems. Share your wonder, "Wow! Look what you made with these simple shapes!" You help children focus by asking them to communicate their intentions and describe their actions. You can also make suggestions as necessary, e.g., "What if you tried…?"

Help children see the connections between what they are doing on the computer and what they draw, build, or create in other classroom areas. When appropriate, call attention to mathematical concepts in the computer programs and use mathematical vocabulary. Taking time to explore the computer program, yourself, will increase your awareness of its mathematical possibilities.

Number and Operations

How many bugs will you put in that box?

Do you want more?

If you added one more piece here, how many would there be altogether? What if you took one piece away?

Can you find another way to show five?

Geometry and Spatial Sense

All of your shapes have curved sides.

Are there any other ways that you could put those shapes together?

Your creature can go backward, forward, up, and down, just like you do.

Hmm, how do you think you can get there?

Measurement

Wow! They're getting bigger and bigger and bigger!

How many of those little boxes do you think will fit in this box?

Which shape can you cover with the most squares?

Don't forget to set the timer so you know when your turn at the computer is over.

Patterns (Algebra)

What an interesting pattern!

Tell me your plan.

I see you created a snake with shapes. You made a pattern! Will you read it for me?

Do you see any patterns in this photo?

Data Analysis

Which things do you think go together?

Are you looking for shapes that are the same or different?

What if you want a different color?

Mathematical Process Skills (Reasoning, Problem Solving, Communicating, Connecting, and Representing)

Hmmm, I wonder why that happened. What do you think?

You figured out your problem. Will you show me how you did it?

How did you make that color?

Would you like to see whether we can find some information about that on the Internet?

If you print a copy of that, do you think you could make one like it out of blocks?

Observing Children's Progress

As children explore the computer and use various software programs, look for these indications of mathematics development and learning:

- counting
- recognizing numerals
- copying or creating patterns
- recognizing, matching, naming, describing, and/or drawing shapes
- comparing or matching size (e.g., choosing the shoes that fit characters in *Millie's Math House*)
- sorting figures by color, shape, or size
- problem solving (e.g., figuring out what icons mean and how to use the mouse)
- showing a friend how to get a desired result
- explaining a process
- creating representations
- making home–school connections

Mathematics Outdoors

Mathematics can be an integral and important part of most outdoor play experiences: counting each rung while climbing the slide's ladder, considering which tree is tallest, noting the striped pattern on a caterpillar, or crawling through a tunnel. Mathematics vocabulary easily becomes a part of outdoor conversations. For example, children talk about who will ride the tricycle *first*, *second*, or *third*; announce who pedals *faster*; explain how they wove *around* traffic *cones*, or tell the teacher about the duration of a friend's turn with a new toy.

Organized games such as hopscotch encourage children to use numbers, while "Mother, May I?" requires that they have an understanding of both measurement and directional concepts (e.g., "May I take two giant steps?" "No, you may take four baby steps backwards.") Here are more examples of how children's outdoor explorations relate to *The Creative Curriculum for Preschool* objectives for mathematics development and learning.

Examples of What a Child Might Do	Examples of Related Objectives for Development and Learning
Plant one pea in each small hole in the garden	Objective 20. Uses number concepts and operations a. Counts
Look at the jungle gym and say without counting, "Five kids are already playing on that, so I'll wait."	Objective 20. Uses number concepts and operations b. Quantifies
Hop to the hopscotch square with a *10* and say, "I hopped on 10 squares."	Objective 20. Uses number concepts and operations c. Connects numerals with their quantities
Say, "Look! I'm above everybody!" when she is on top of the climber	Objective 21. Explores and describes spatial relationships and shapes a. Understands spatial relationships
Point to a yield sign and say, "That's a triangle."	Objective 21. Explores and describes spatial relationships and shapes b. Understands shapes
Stand in the sunlight and say, "I'm bigger than my shadow"	Objective 22. Compares and measures
Notice the pattern made by wet boots on the sidewalk	Objective 23. Demonstrates knowledge of patterns

Mathematics Materials for the Outdoors

Well-planned outdoor spaces provide opportunities for children to make many mathematical connections. *The Creative Curriculum for Preschool, Volume 2: Interest Areas* provides additional information about setting up and equipping the outdoors to maximize learning. The chart below suggests books and materials to encourage problem solving and encourage children to find their own answers to mathematical questions related to nature.

Materials

equipment of varying sizes (e.g., small, medium, large balls; streamers or ribbons of various lengths)

magnifying glasses and binoculars for observing things near and far

materials to create an obstacle course or equipment that invites children to go over, under, around, and through

standard and nonstandard measuring tools (e.g., rulers, yardstick/meter stick, measuring tapes, craft sticks, connecting cubes, and plastic links)

nature guides (plant and animal identification books)

rain gauge

wind sock or weather vane

sundial

materials for outdoor sand and water mathematical explorations (see "Mathematics in the Sand and Water Area")

muffin tins, egg cartons, or ice cube trays for sorting collections

traffic signs related to direction, speed, and right-of-way (e.g., one way, U-turn, stop, speed limit, and yield)

clipboards, paper, and writing materials (for creating representations and drawing from a variety of perspectives)

Suggested Books

(Titles preceded by an asterisk are included in the Teaching Strategies Children's Book Collection.)

At the Edge of the Woods (Cynthia Cotton)

*Bounce (Doreen Cronin and Scott Menchin)

Bugs Are Insects (Anne Rockwell)

Countdown to Spring: An Animal Counting Book (Janet Schulman)

Counting on the Woods: A Poem (George Ella Lyon)

Counting Wildflowers (Bruce McMillan)

Deep Down Underground (Olivier Dunrea)

Dots, Spots, Speckles, and Stripes (Tana Hoban)

*A Grand Old Tree (Mary Newell DePalma)

Icky Bug Counting Book (Jerry Pallotta)

Suggested Books, continued

Inch by Inch (Leo Lionni)

*Just Like Josh Gibson
(Angela Johnson)

Millions of Snowflakes
(Mary McKenna Siddals)

Over, Under, Through (Tana Hoban)

Shapes, Shapes, Shapes (Tana Hoban)

Turtle Splash!: Countdown at the Pond
(Cathryn Falwell)

What's Up? What's Down?
(Lola M. Schaefer)

Ten Flashing Fireflies
(Philemon Sturges)

*The Wildlife ABC & 1 2 3: A Nature
Alphabet and Counting Book*
(Jan Thornhill)

Wonderful Worms (Linda Glaser)

Using the Outdoors to Teach Mathematics

Respond to children's calls to "Look how high I am!" or "Look at the line the plane made in the sky!" with simple comments or questions. You might say, "Wow, you're on the highest rung! You're even taller than I am," or "I wonder what made that line. What do you think?" By using mathematical language in your casual conversations with children, you help them develop important mathematical process skills, understandings, and vocabulary. More importantly, you demonstrate an enthusiasm for learning that is sure to be contagious. Here are examples of what you might say and ask:

Number and Operations

"You're on the first rung of the climber. How high do you think you'll climb? Up to there, the fourth rung?"

"Will you collect all of the balls and put them in this cart?"

"How many bugs do you have in your bug box?"

"Do you have more red leaves or more yellow leaves?"

"Yes, Setsuko, our tricycle track does look like the numeral *8*."

Geometry and Spatial Sense

"Are you ready? When I say, 'Go,' run around the tree, through the tunnel, and then straight back here."

"Remember to keep the tricycles inside the area marked by the orange cones."

"Do you get dizzy, going around and around on the merry-go-round?"

"Can you find something on our playground that is shaped like a can?"

"How does that jump rope rhyme go? 'Teddy bear, teddy bear, turn around. Teddy bear, teddy bear, touch the ground…'"

Measurement

"How many footsteps does it take to go from the climber to the slide? Will you take big steps or small steps?"

"Can you find a bush that's just as tall as you are? …that's taller? …that's shorter?"

"How wide is this tree? Can you reach around it? What if we hold hands with each other? Can we reach around it now?"

"Let's check the rain gauge to see how much it rained last night."

"How can we find out how deep the snow is? Do you think some places have more snow than other places?"

Patterns (Algebra)

"Do you see the pattern that the tricycle tire made when it came out of the puddle?"

"Look at this footprint. Do you know who made it? How can you find out?"

"That's an interesting pattern on the caterpillar. How would you describe it?"

"Would you like to take photos of patterns we see on the playground? Let me know when you see one."

"Follow me back to the classroom. Hop, hop, jump; hop, hop, jump; hop, hop, jump…"

Data Analysis

"You found two kinds of flowers: dandelions and buttercups. What's different about them? How are they the same?"

"You found a stone that writes like chalk. Do you think other stones will make marks on the pavement?"

"Can you put the leaves shaped like this one on this tray and put the leaves shaped like that one on that tray?"

"Can you put a mark on your clipboard for every step it takes to get from the door to the slide? Then we can do the same thing from the door to the climber and see which is farther away."

Mathematical Process Skills (Reasoning, Problem Solving, Communicating, Connecting, and Representing)

"How can you tell it's windy?"

"There are not enough tricycles for everyone to have one. What can we do so that everyone who wants a turn on that tricycle will get one?"

"You learned to swing all by yourself. Tell me how you learned that."

"You drew pictures of clouds! They remind me of the pictures in the book *It Looked Like Spilt Milk*. Would you like to make yours into a book?"

"The seeds we planted are starting to sprout. How can we keep track of how much they grow each week?"

Observing Children's Progress

As children play and explore outdoors, look for these indications of mathematics development and learning:

- counting (e.g., collections of objects; quantifying during games and activities)
- using ordinal numbers (e.g., *first, second, third*)
- using terms such as *some, all, more, less*
- recognizing, describing, copying, or creating patterns
- using positional words such as *over, under, in front of, next to, behind*
- measuring with standard units (e.g., ruler or tape measure) or nonstandard units (e.g., arm's-length, footsteps, or connecting cubes)
- using comparative terms (e.g., *taller–shorter; higher–lower,* and *smaller–larger*)
- recognizing or describing two- and three-dimensional shapes
- discussing similarities and differences
- collecting, organizing, and representing data (e.g., sorting and classifying collections of natural objects)

Appendix

**The Creative Curriculum for Preschool:
Selected Objectives for Development
and Learning**
Mathematics
(Objectives 20–23)

**Glossary: Two- and
Three-Dimensional Figures**

Mathematics (Objectives 20–23)

Objective 20 Uses number concepts and operations

a. Counts

Not Yet	1	2	3	4	5	6	7	8	9
		Verbally counts (not always in the correct order) • Says, "One, two, ten" as she pretends to count		**Verbally counts to 10; counts up to five objects accurately, using one number name for each object** • Counts to ten when playing "Hide and Seek" • Counts out four scissors and puts them at the table		**Verbally counts to 20; counts 10–20 objects accurately; knows the last number states how many in all; tells what number (1–10) comes next in order by counting** • Counts to twenty while walking across room • Counts ten plastic worms and says, "I have ten worms." • When asked, "What comes after six?" says, "One, two, three, four, five, six, seven...seven."		**Uses number names while counting to 100; counts 30 objects accurately; tells what number comes before and after a specified number up to 20** • Counts twenty-eight steps to the cafeteria • When asked what comes after fifteen, says "Sixteen."	

b. Quantifies

Not Yet	1	2	3	4	5	6	7	8	9
		Demonstrates understanding of the concepts of one, two, and more • Says, "More apple," to indicate he wants more pieces than given • Takes two crackers when prompted, "Take two crackers."		**Recognizes and names the number of items in a small set (up to five) instantly; combines and separates up to five objects and describes the parts** • Looks at the sand table and says instantly, without counting, "There are three children at the table." • Says, "I have four cubes. Two are red, and two are blue." • Puts three bunnies in the box with the two bears. Counts and says, "Now I have five."		**Makes sets of 6–10 objects and then describes the parts; identifies which part has more, less, or the same (equal); counts all or counts on to find out how many** • Says, "I have eight big buttons, and you have eight little buttons. We have the same." • Tosses ten puff balls at the hoop. When three land outside she says, "More went inside." • Puts two dominoes together, says, "Five dots," and counts on "Six, seven, eight. Eight dots all together."		**Uses a variety of strategies (counting objects or fingers, counting on, or counting back) to solve problems with more than 10 objects** • Uses ladybug counters to solve the problem, "You had eight ladybugs. Two flew away. How many ladybugs are left?" • Says, "I have ten cars. I left two at Grandma's, so now I have ten, nine, eight left." • Uses two-sided counters to determine different number combinations for fourteen	

Objective 20 Uses number concepts and operations

c. Connects numerals with their quantities

Not Yet	1	2	3	4	5	6	7	8	9
		Recognizes and names a few numerals • Points to the 1 when the teacher says, "Where is the numeral 1?" • Notices numerals around the room and calls some of them by name		**Identifies numerals to 5 by name and connects each to counted objects** • Says, "Five" as she attaches five clothespins to the 5 card • Tells her friend, "That's a 3, and there are three puppies on this page."		**Identifies numerals to 10 by name and connects each to counted objects** • Shouts, "Seven," and jumps seven times when the teacher holds up the number 7 card • Says, "I put nine buttons in the 9 box."		**Identifies numerals to 20 by name and connects each to counted objects** • Says, "Kaufee put the 12 card and twelve beads on his necklace." • Says, "I drew fifteen flowers to go on page 15 of our number book."	

Objective 21 Explores and describes spatial relationships and shapes

a. Understands spatial relationships

Not Yet	1	2	3	4	5	6	7	8	9
		Follows simple directions related to position (in, on, under, up, down) • Follows teacher's directions to put the trash in the can • Raises hands up and down as the song directs		**Follows simple directions related to proximity (beside, between, next to)** • Follows teacher's direction to put the cup next to the plate • Sits beside her friend when he says, "Sit between me and Laura."		**Uses and responds appropriately to positional words indicating location, direction, and distance** • Says, "Look for the surprise behind the tree." • Moves game piece backward when playmate gives directions		**Uses and makes simple sketches, models, or pictorial maps to locate objects** • Constructs a map of the play yard using landscape toys • Uses a map of the classroom to find the hidden treasure	

b. Understands shapes

Not Yet	1	2	3	4	5	6	7	8	9
		Matches two identical shapes • Puts a circular puzzle piece in the circular space • Places shapes in a shape-sorting box		**Identifies a few basic shapes (circle, square, triangle)** • Looks at a wheel and says, "A circle." • Names shape pieces as he puts them on a shape lotto card		**Describes basic two- and three-dimensional shapes by using own words; recognizes basic shapes when they are presented in a new orientation** • Says, "It's a ball 'cause it rolls." • Puts hand in feely box and says, "It has three sides and three points. It's a triangle."		**Shows that shapes remain the same when they are turned, flipped, or slid; breaks apart or combines shapes to create different shapes and sizes** • Says, "It's still a triangle no matter how you turn it." • Cuts apart a rectangle to make two squares	

Objective 22 Compares and measures

Not Yet	1	2	3	4	5	6	7	8	9
		Makes simple comparisons between two objects • Pours sand or water from one container to another • Indicates which ball is bigger when shown a tennis ball and a beach ball		**Compares and orders a small set of objects as appropriate according to size, length, weight, area, or volume; knows usual sequence of basic daily events and a few ordinal numbers** • Puts blocks side by side in order of length • Says, "We go outside after lunch." • Lays two short blocks on top of a long block to see if it's the same length • Responds, "You're second to use the computer."		**Uses multiples of the same unit to measure; uses numbers to compare; knows the purpose of standard measuring tools** • Measures by using paper clips, cubes, string, hands, feet or other objects • Measures block tower with linking cubes and says, "I made mine fifteen cubes high!!" • Stands on scale while pretending to be in a doctor's office		**Uses measurement words and some standard measurement tools accurately; uses ordinal numbers from *first to tenth*** • Says, "We need two cups of flour and one cup of salt to make dough." • Says, "If I add three more tiles to this side of the scale, they'll be the same." • Looks at the clock and says, "It's 12 o'clock. It's time for lunch."	

Objective 23 Demonstrates knowledge of patterns

Not Yet	1	2	3	4	5	6	7	8	9
		Shows interest in simple patterns in everyday life		**Copies simple repeating patterns**		**Extends and creates simple repeating patterns**		**Recognizes, creates, and explains more complex repeating and simple growing patterns**	
		• Notices that a special song is played whenever it is time to clean up		• Beats a drum as the teacher does, e.g., loud, soft; loud, soft; loud, soft; etc.		• Makes a repeating movement pattern, e.g., stomp, stomp, clap, clap; stomp, stomp, clap, clap; stomp, stomp, clap, clap; etc.		• Describes even numbers, e.g., 2, 4, 6, 8, etc., as "skipping" every other number on a 100's chart	
		• Points to the tiles in the bathroom and says, "They go this way, that way, this way, that way."		• Strings beads as her friend does, e.g., red, blue, blue; red, blue, blue; red, blue, blue; etc.		• When shown pattern of cubes, e.g., red, blue, blue, red; red, blue, blue, red; etc., adds to it correctly		• Says, "If I add one to three, it's the next number: four. If I add one to four, it's the next number: five."	
								• Extends a growing pattern by adding one cube like a staircase, e.g., 1 cube, 2 cubes, 3 cubes, 4 cubes, etc.	

Glossary

Two-Dimensional Figures

circle: a collection of points on a plane where each point is the same distance from a fixed point called the center

polygon: a closed figure made of line segments

regular polygon: a polygon whose sides and angles are all the same length

triangle: a three-sided polygon

quadrilateral: a four-sided polygon

trapezoid: a four-sided polygon with only one pair of parallel sides

rectangle: a four-sided polygon with all right angles

square rectangle: a special rectangle having equal length sides with all right angles

parallelogram: a four-sided polygon with two pairs of parallel sides

rhombus: a four-sided polygon with all four sides of equal length

pentagon: a five-sided polygon

hexagon: a six-sided polygon

Three-Dimensional Figures

 sphere: a three-dimensional figure with all points equal distance from the center

 cube: a three-dimensional figure with six equal square faces

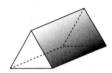 **triangular prism:** a three-dimensional figure with congruent triangular-shaped bases, that is, both bases are the same size and shape

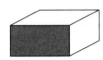 **rectangular prism:** a three-dimensional figure with congruent rectangular-shaped bases, that is, both bases are the same size and shape

 cone: a three-dimensional figure with a circular base and a single vertex

 square pyramid: a three-dimensional figure with a square base and four triangular sides

 cylinder: a figure with two congruent circular parallel bases, that is, both bases are the same size and shape

 triangular pyramid: a three-dimensional figure with a triangular base and three triangular faces

References

Baroody, A. J. (2004). The developmental bases for early childhood number and operations standards. In D. H. Clements, J. Sarama, & A. Dibiase (Eds.), *Engaging young children in mathematics* (pp. 173–220). Mahwah, NJ: Lawrence Erlbaum Associates.

Carpenter, T. P., & Levi, L. (1999, April). *Developing conceptions of algebraic reasoning in the primary grades.* Paper presented at the meeting of the American Educational Research Association, Montreal, Canada.

Clements, D. H. (1999). Geometry and spatial thinking in young children. In J. V. Copley (Ed.), *Mathematics in the early years* (pp. 66–79). Reston, VA: National Council of Teachers of Mathematics.

Clements, D. H. (2003, September). *Good beginnings in mathematics: Linking a national vision to state action.* New York: Carnegie Corporation.

Clements, D. H. (2004). Geometric and spatial thinking in early childhood education. In D. H. Clements, J. Sarama, & A. Dibiase (Eds.), *Engaging young children in mathematics* (pp. 267–298). Mahwah, NJ: Lawrence Erlbaum Associates.

Clements, D. H., Battista, M. T., Sarama, J., & Swaminathan, S. (1997). Development of students' spatial thinking in a unit on geometric motions and area. *The Elementary School Journal, 98*(2), 171–186.

Clements, D. H., Swaminathan, S., Hannibal, M. A. Z., & Sarama, J. (1999). Young children's concepts of shape. *Journal for Research in Mathematics Education, 30,* 192–212.

Copley, J. V. (2000). *The young child and mathematics.* Washington D.C.: National Association for the Education of the Young Child and National Council of Teachers of Mathematics.

Copley, J. V. (2004). The early childhood collaborative: A professional development model to communicate and implement the standards. In D. H. Clements, J. Sarama, and A. Dibiase (Eds.), *Engaging young children in mathematics* (pp. 401–414). Mahwah, NJ: Lawrence Erbaum Associates.

Copley, J. V. (Ed.). (2004). *Showcasing mathematics for the young child: Activities for three-, four-, and five-year-olds.* Reston, VA: National Council of Teachers of Mathematics.

Copley, J. V. (2005). *Measuring with young children.* Paper presented at the International Conference for the Education of the Young Child, Madrid, Spain.

Copley, J. V., & Hawkins, J. (2005). *Interim report of C3 coaching grant: Mathematics professional development.*

Friel, S. N., Curcio, F. R., & Bright, G. W. (2001). Making sense of graphs: Critical factors influencing comprehension and instructional implications. *Journal for Research in Mathematics Education, 32,* 124–158.

Gelman, R., & Gallistel, C. R. (1978). *The child's understanding of number.* Cambridge, MA: Harvard University Press.

Kilpatrick, J., Swafford, J., & Findell, B. (2001). *Adding it up: Helping children learn mathematics.* Washington, DC: National Academy Press.

National Council of Teachers of Mathematics. (2006). *Curriculum focal points for prekindergarten through grade 8 mathematics: A quest for coherence.* Reston, VA: Author.

National Council of Teachers of Mathematics. (2000). *Principles and standards for school mathematics.* Reston, VA: Author.

Piaget, J., & Inhelder, B. (1967). *The child's conception of space* (F. J. Langdon & J. L. Lunzer, Trans.). New York: Norton.

Piaget, J., Inhelder, B., & Szeminska, A. (1952). *The child's conception of geometry.* London: Routledge & Kegan Paul.

Russell, S. J. (1991). Counting noses and scary things: Children construct their ideas about data. In D. Vere-Jones (Ed.), *Proceedings of the third international conference on teaching statistics* (pp. 158–164). Voorburg, Netherlands: International Statistical Institute.

Siegler, R. S., & Robinson, M. (1982). The development of numerical understanding. In H. W. Reese & L. P. Lipsitt (Eds.), *Advances in child development and behavior* (pp. 241–312). New York: Academic Press.

Starkey, P. (1992). The early development of numerical reasoning. *Cognition and Instruction, 43,* 93–126.

Steffe, L. P. & Cobb, P. (1988). *Construction of arithmetical meanings and strategies.* New York: Springer-Verlag.

Van Hiele, P. M. (1986). *Structure and insight: A theory of mathematics education.* Orlando, FL: Academic Press.